LEGALIZE

THE ONLY WAY TO COMBAT DRUGS

Max Rendall

D1418241

STACEY
INTERNATIONAL

Legalize

STACEY INTERNATIONAL

128 Kensington Church Street

London W8 4BH

Tel: +44 (0)20 7221 7166; Fax: +44 (0)20 7792 9288

Email: info@stacey-international.co.uk

www.stacey-international.co.uk

ISBN: 9781906768652

CIP Data: A catalogue record for this book is available from the British Library

1 3 5 7 9 0 8 6 4 2

Printed in the UK

Contents

Author's Preface

As a young doctor working in a casualty department in a central London hospital at the very end of the 1950s, I came across small numbers of addicts. They were not derelicts, and seemed much like their more sober fellow citizens. Throughout most of my professional life I was aware of the occasional patient who was an addict, but this was of more concern to anaesthetists than to surgeons. In retirement, looking for something to retain my contact with patients and medicine, I had the opportunity to work in a pioneering clinic treating addicts, initially as a surgeon inserting Naltrexone implants, which block the effect of opiates on the brain. I soon became further involved, both with the care and management of patients, and in the politics of drug policy.

I also had some first hand experience of the struggle against heroin in my own family. I watched impotently as this most seductive of sirens took over a young life, and how, with great character and courage, he was able to wrest control again from this terrible curse. It was a humbling experience.

Introduction

The drugs problem has two heads – criminality and addiction. Firm concerted compliance with the cause for which this book argues will cut off one head: the use (or abuse) of drugs by adults will no longer be a crime anywhere in the world; and drugs will be available, under state supervision, at a price which undercuts any incentive for black-marketeers.

The other head is the readiness of the few of every generation to be tempted into recourse for mood-changing drugs to the point of addiction. The loss of its criminalized fellow, the more recent head, will not increase that temptation. It could very well diminish it. That lure has been with us immemorially. When God identified a single tree in Eden whose fruit was prohibited to the First Man, He made it compellingly alluring.

Many know the truth of this. Yet nowhere is a policy of multilateral legalization of all drugs on the agenda of any international forum with the power to implement it or the authority to advocate it successfully. And nowhere yet has a national political leader of significant global authority stepped forward to champion such legalization.

Meanwhile we endure the appalling consequences stemming from such political funk. Drug-funded international terrorism has become an issue of urgent concern all over the world. Its associated corruption and violence threatens the cohesiveness and governability of nations, and even, in a few cases, the very existence of some small countries. Attempting to contain this fear and violence costs inordinate sums of money. The source of all this is the unimaginable profits to be made from the international trade in drugs, and trafficking to the user, whether addict or recreational.

For much of the twentieth century individual nations sought ways to deal with their domestic drug problems. Policies have varied, but their constant has been prohibition, egged on and encouraged, and if necessary bullied, by the United States. As we shall see, this policy has overseen explosive growth in drug taking throughout the world, and the ubiquitous availability of affordable drugs on our streets. It has failed irredeemably. The market for drugs is lucrative, extraordinarily so, and it is run by criminal enterprises which will fight tooth and nail to retain it. All efforts to dislodge them have failed, and will continue to fail wherever prohibition persists.

Policies have included attempts to destroy narcotic crops in producer countries, or paying them not to grow them, to intercept drugs in transit, to stop drugs entering the country of destination, to sharpen ever further the vigilance by police against drug dealers at all levels, to the making of mere possession of drugs a criminal act. The law has been deployed with virtually no deterrent effect, and has blighted the lives of many young people, victims of addiction or simply curious and foolish, to no advantage. There are momentary successes, but the vast bulk of drugs do make it across our borders to be sold by criminals to users on the streets of our cities, towns and villages.

One strategy that has not been tried is the one by which profits from drug dealing would be abolished at a stroke, the incentive to deal in drugs would vanish, and with drugs available on demand inexpensively at licensed dealers, acquisitive crime to pay for them would cease. The way to achieve this is to make all currently illegal drugs legal, on an agreed date, everywhere. From being immensely valuable illegal contraband, the constituent element in various drugs will have become another agricultural product, freely bought and sold on the markets of the world. Regulated markets would emerge, with appropriate limitations on access, and even an option on raising taxes as on alcohol.

Formal accessibility to drugs surely carries a risk of some contracting a drug habit who had previously been deterred by its associated criminality. Yet any such risk is surely outweighed by the certain elimination of international crime, violence, bribery and terrorism. Today's international situation renders the option urgent. To be choosing between two evils, one certain and one speculative, does not excuse inaction.

This book pleads for a break with the past. We need to draw a line under the mistakes of the last half-century and longer. Prohibition handed the second biggest international trade, worth about $500 billion a year, to the criminal fraternity on a plate. Let us but spend a fraction of the enormous savings of the cost of prohibition on treating addicts.

What we therefore wish to see is:

- ⊕ Simultaneous legalization of all currently illegal drugs throughout the world.

- ⊕ On the appointed day it would no longer be a concern of the police or the law for an individual to possess such drugs for his or her own use, or to use them.

- ⊕ This change should be organized by, and under the leadership of, the United Nations, which alone has the structure and authority to sponsor such radical action. It took the comprehensive role in fostering the 1961, 1971 and 1988 Conventions on illegal drugs, psychotropic drugs, and the trafficking of drugs internationally.

- ⊕ National governments should be charged with the responsibility of putting in place a controlled and licensed market for drugs, at fixed moderate prices, setting enforceable age limits on access to the different drugs, labelling with the potential consequences of their use.

- ⊕ Prices should initially not be determined by pure market forces, but controlled centrally at levels to forestall black-marketeering, and therefore not subject to arbitrage.

- ⊕ Governments would be free, within an agreed framework, to make their own arrangements. The pattern of drug use varies between countries, and local arrangements must be free to respond to this. Variations of this kind will, over time, test different models of care provision, and so allow best practice to emerge.

- ⊕ Transitional arrangements in poor rural drug-producing countries, like Afghanistan and some Central and South American nations, may be necessary. A precipitous fall in the market price of poppies or coca leaf would have to be managed to obviate destitution among the farmers, provoking potential political unrest. This would be the responsibility of the United Nations.

The title of this book is the single word 'Legalize'. Let there be no misunderstanding as to its precise meaning. In this context it is a technical term which means that the possession of currently illegal drugs for personal use, and their consumption would henceforth be legal. Neither such possession or use would be a matter of concern to the police or the law. Were drug use to result in public nuisance, it would be dealt with by the civil law, just as it is now in the case of alcohol-related misbehaviour. Legalization differs from decriminalization, such as is now in force in Portugal and a few other countries. 'Decriminalization' has come to mean no more than that possession (usually of a specific drug, such as cannabis) for personal use, and consumption, though technically illegal, are not considered *criminal* acts.

Some argue that decriminalization is enough, it is manifestly not so. The supply of decriminalized drugs remains in the hands of criminals, who determine the quality and prices, and are still incentivized to 'push' drugs. All that has resulted in today's Portugal, for example, is a legal market in illegal goods.

Legalization is not, as is often characterized, a soft or libertarian gesture. It is a specific and essential prerequisite to depossessing criminals of the market of drugs, with all the benefits that would bring to addicts, societies and the nations of the world.

There is nothing good about drug taking. Yet it is there, and among some an insatiable appetite will persist. No one can suppose that drugs can be made to go away. Let us work with these realities, regulate and legalize.

Tom Stacey
Max Rendall
August 2011

1   The Problem

Drugs have been around for a very long time. There is archaeological evidence of our ancestors using opium in 4200 BC,[1] and in all probability long before that. Until about fifty years ago the use of drugs for non-medical and pleasurable purposes was, in Britain and the United States, confined to a very few hundred people posing no threat or problem to society. Today the streets of our cities, towns and even villages are awash with drugs because they find a ready market. Illegal drugs are now one of the biggest and most pressing social issues for governments throughout the world. It is a problem that is corroding society, with implications for social policy, policing, the criminal justice system, health, education and the cohesiveness of society. Furthermore, there is wide disagreement as to how this issue might be addressed – a state of affairs that favours inaction and the persistence of outdated and failed policies.

It is the purpose of the book to review this situation, and to propose how key new thinking can transform the issues engendered by the appeal and consumption of drugs. The issues are contentious, and there is often little experience to guide further action. Opposing arguments take refuge in notions of what is 'right', which entail deeply held and individual convictions, and on what is electorally acceptable. What we seek is a pragmatic solution to a range of practical problems. Drug policy is dangerous territory to enter, but the *status quo* is no longer sustainable.

There is nothing good about the drugs currently classified as illegal. But they are here, and no one can believe that they can be made to go away. We must, therefore, work with these realities. The present ubiquitous availability of drugs has developed in spite of prohibition, as a consequence of uncontrolled markets run by criminals, and the unquenchable appetite in society for their use. The policy of legalization is determined to abolish the criminal market and put in its place a regulated and controlled one. The legalization of drugs is a necessary prerequisite, since it is not possible to have a legal market in illegal goods.

Legalization is not a doctrinal or libertarian stance or end itself. Nor is it a silver bullet such as might prove to be 'the answer' to the problem of drug abuse. It should be seen as an important step in ameliorating the harms that drug use and production currently bring to any society. It would lead to a tightly controlled, internationally implemented system for the sale of mind-altering drugs, which ensures safety, harm reduction, assured and controlled strengths and purities, guaranteed sterility when appropriate and proper labelling. Furthermore, regular trading forces would determine prices, regulated by governments at a level which eliminates any chance of a black market. We have many years' experience of running such markets. Legalization is often misrepresented as a policy that would 'liberalize' or 'relax' the control of drugs. This is the opposite of the truth.

Between the two opposite positions of prohibition and legalization lie a number of arguments. There is a libertarian principle which enjoys much support. It states that citizens should be allowed to do what they want, so long as they are adults and know the risks, they do no harm to others, and they impose no costs on the public purse. This is discussed more fully in Chapter 7. Some prohibitionists have a moral basis that legitimizes their beliefs. They hold that it is wrong to take any psychoactive or intoxicating drug, other than for a strictly necessary medical indication. For anyone who holds this view, prohibition is a likely choice. Morality is about right and wrong or good and evil. But here we have a difficulty: concepts of good and evil are not always enforceable by laws.

On right and wrong who is to be the arbiter? The individual citizen? A wise man paid to decide? The majority view? The government? But moral purity has a price. The holders of such views must take their share of responsibility for the consequences of prohibition. Murder, violence, corruption, property crime and the criminalization, and in many cases the imprisonment of hundreds of thousands of their fellow citizens, are all a direct result of the illegality of drugs, not of drugs themselves. That is a heavy burden to bear.

The world today faces a pandemic of drug taking, and there are very few people who are not exposed at some time to its contagion. Throughout the world hundreds of millions have at some time in their lives taken drugs.[2] They have done so because they enjoy the effects, whether these be to insulate them for a short time from the worries and pressures of their lives, to give them energy and a feeling of omnipotence, to enhance their perceptions, to induce relaxation, or to confer an ease and sociability which they do not otherwise feel. These can be seductive motives. Those who cannot concede this are perhaps confusing the feeling induced by drugs with disapproval of the illegal market from which they are obtained. Are they equally disapproving of similar feelings engendered as a consequence of drinking alcohol or smoking tobacco – both accepted and legal features of many people's normal lives?

What is it, therefore, that has happened in the last fifty years or so to make illegal drugs such an acute and pressing problem of concern to the government of every country in the world? It is simply the scale of drug taking, and its ubiquity in all corners of the societies of the world. And, at the present time, in the wake of drugs comes corruption and violence on a scale never seen before. Provable facts about any aspect of illegal drugs are difficult to come by; but it is calculated that the production and distribution of illegal drugs is the second largest industry in the world by value, after the arms trade. Furthermore, not a penny is raised for tax.

Numbers are almost unimaginable. The industry is believed to generate $500 billion every year, and it 'should' be paying tax to the nations of the world in the order of hundreds of millions of dollars. And missed tax revenue is only one of the costs of illegal drugs. As we shall see, the nations of the world spend many billions of dollars trying, with singularly little success, to stop the growing, processing and distribution of drugs, in addition to criminal justice costs and those associated with the consequences of drug-related crime and harms to health.

Throughout the nineteenth century opium preparations were to be found in every household. They were used for a wide range of ailments – they were effective painkillers, and they suppressed coughing at a time when tuberculosis of the lungs was common. This caused a dry, relentless and sleep-depriving cough, which kept not only the unfortunate sufferer awake, but the rest of the family as well. Opium was also a remarkably effective cure for diarrhoea, which was common in a time of uncertain water supplies and poor food hygiene.

The consumption of small amounts of opium or laudanum (opium dissolved in brandy) was a common restorative after a week's industrial drudgery in the new cotton mills in the North, or the grinding physical labour of digging ditches in the Isle of Ely.[3] It was much cheaper than beer, and the practice was widespread. It is said that in some parts of the country brewers actually put small amounts of opium into their beer, but it is difficult to find proof of this. Children were often given opium-containing draughts to get them to sleep, or to sedate them while their parents were out at work. There were many to choose from like 'Mother Bailey's quieting syrup' or 'Copp's baby friend'.[4] When used in moderation little or no harm resulted, though there were a few unfortunates who became dependent, which they only realized when they became ill if they did not have a little more. During these years there was a free and legal market in opium, and the needs of the family were supplied by corner shops everywhere. But drug taking was never confined to the working classes. Throughout the eighteenth and nineteenth centuries and beyond, a small procession of public figures from all walks of life have passed before the gaze of history. The writer Thomas De Quincey is the best known, and his book, *The Confessions of an English Opium-Eater*, published in 1821, quickly became a classic, and influenced many other literary figures.

Coleridge, George Crabbe, Elizabeth Barrett Browning, Edgar Alan Poe, Wilkie Collins, Baudelaire and Aleister Crowley were all dependent opiate users. Many other writers and artists were familiar with drugs of one kind or another. These included William Butler Yeats, Havelock Ellis, Martin Heidegger, Jean Cocteau, William Burroughs, Alexander Trocchi, Claude Debussy, Eric Satie, Alfred Jarry, Salvador Dali, Pablo Picasso, Aldous Huxley, Ernst Jünger, Colette, Enid Bagnold, and the vast majority of pop musicians since the 1960s. Other distinguished or notorious figures included Clive of India, William Wilberforce, Bismarck, the French neurologist Charcot, Sigmund Freud, Hermann Göring, Adolph Hitler, the father of American surgery William Halstead, and Yves Saint Laurent. All were, at some time in their lives, familiar with narcotic drugs. And there will have been regiments, or more likely armies, of people whose names we shall never know. Queen Victoria is said to have been treated with cannabis for period pains, with good effect.

In 1868 the Pharmacy Act confined the sale of opium products to chemists' shops, but this was largely a response to continued lobbying by pharmaceutical interests to ensure that only they could sell such medicines, rather than an attempt to control their use. The price of opium went up a little, but not much else changed until the early years of the twentieth century, when the sale and labelling of such preparations and those containing the then new cocaine, were increasingly controlled by the 1908 Poisons and Pharmacy Act. This culminated in the Defence of the Realm Act Regulation 40B in July 1916, enacted as a result of suspicions during the Great War that cocaine was being distributed by London prostitutes to the troops on leave. This provision essentially stopped the free and legal market in narcotics.

The 1920s and 1930s were a time of stability in the use of illegal drugs in Britain. There were about 350 addicts known to the Home Office, mostly professional people like doctors, nurses, pharmacists and vets, who had some access to drugs. There were also very small numbers of people, usually depressives or neurotics, who became dependent on injected morphine given to them by their doctors. In addition one can read in biographies of the tiny numbers of well-off bohemians who were occasional users of morphine or cocaine, and these trends are reflected in the literature of the times. Morphine in particular was expensive and outside the reach of all but the best off.

After the sacrifices and austerities of the Second World War, the young of America and the rest of the Western world were to be caught up in a new mood of self-liberation, license and emotional daring in which experimentation with drugs played a seminal role. In 1954, Aldous Huxley published *The Doors of Perception*, describing his own experiences with the Mexican drug mescaline, and introducing an element of respectability to drug use. The Beat Generation was emerging on the West Coast of the United States, with luminaries such as the poet Allen Ginsberg, the novelist Jack Kerouac and the psychologist Timothy Leary, all exemplars of a drug-taking subculture. Their inheritors were the hippies of the 1960s and the new rock and pop groups that this period produced.

Until about 1960 the world of illegal drug abuse in Britain was small in scale. But things were changing. Addiction to drugs was becoming a problem. In the late 1960s 'Treatment Centres' were set up by the government which prescribed heroin, initially intravenously, then orally, and then ceased to dispense heroin in favour of methadone. These were initially a shambles, with policies guided by the fashions of the moment, and much of their very generous prescriptions found its way onto the black market, which was growing apace. Thefts of narcotic drugs from hospitals and surgeries started to be reported. Criminality was beginning to enter a partnership with drugs, which was later to assume such huge proportions. At this time other drugs were making their way onto the market. Aside from caffeine and alcohol, amphetamines in the form of 'bennies' (Benzedrine inhalers), 'black bombers' and 'purple hearts', as well as barbiturates, were becoming available. Cannabis – still then called Indian hemp – was brought to the party by West Indian musicians.

Other events had an influence on the popularity of heroin taking. In the 1950s the Hong Kong Chinese discovered that heroin could be used without having to inject it intravenously. Hitherto this was the only way to get its full effect, but injection required 'cooking up' in a spoon with an acid, such as lemon juice, to make it dissolve. This was not a sterile process, and it had to be repeated two or three times a day because heroin rapidly decomposes in solution. As with any injected preparation, there was always a danger of overdose, which from time to time proved fatal. 'Chasing the dragon' involves spreading heroin powder, however pure or impure, on kitchen foil and heating it from below with a cigarette lighter. The heroin melts and vaporizes and can be inhaled, with very rapid effects. This avoids the problems of un-sterile injections and the risk of overdose, and is a cheap, safe and easy way to get the effects addicts so avidly desire. Almost overnight the delights of heroin were easily available to a new population who were too fastidious or too incompetent to find a vein three times a day.

Another event affecting London followed the fall of the Shah of Persia in 1979. Smoking a modest amount of opium had been a part of the life of a gentleman in Iran since time immemorial. Many well-off Iranians were faced with the stark choice of remaining in their country under an inhospitable regime, or leaving to make a new life somewhere in the West. Many chose the latter, but they could not take their money with them. It is said that smuggling heroin out of the country solved this problem. Heroin is a high value, low bulk commodity, which proved relatively easy to transport. Furthermore, Iranian heroin melts and vaporizes at a low temperature, and hence was valued and welcomed by the new army of 'dragon chasers'. Like so many things in the world of illicit drugs, it is hard to get concrete evidence that this was true, but it is a plausible and credible story.

In the early days of the heroin epidemic in Britain it was a solely London-based phenomenon. The activities of the few 'script doctors', and later the easy accessibility of the new Treatment Centres, nearly all of which were in London, proved to be a magnet which drew addicts and potential future users to the capital. Gradually, however, drugs started to march out of London, and satellite communities of users sprang up in Crawley, Brighton, the Wirral and the big cities of Scotland.

It was soon on the move again, and progress was inexorable. The new recruits were initially among those who were already users of amphetamines, but soon there were hundreds and even thousands of new users. As we shall see, obtaining accurate figures of drug users is very difficult, and always, for several reasons, an underestimate, but the three or four hundred of the 1950s turned into thousands by the 1980s – an explosive growth rate which brought illegal drugs into the centre of government concern, and forced successive administrations to put in place policies which sought to address all aspects of the problem. Some strands of policy achieved something, but many, even most, were dismally unsuccessful, and one to two even counter-productive.

There are many different drugs which, in varying degree, are attractive to users. They fall into different categories: inebriants like alcohol; hypnotics such as opiates or benzodiazepines; stimulants such as cocaine or amphetamines; and hallucinogens like LSD or 'magic mushrooms'. In some cases a drug may have several actions that cross over these divisions. In Britain, drugs used for pleasure are classified under the 1971 Misuse of Drugs Act as A, B or C, according to the potential harms that can accrue from their use. Recently, however, this basis of classification has been overtaken by some very political decisions, notably the reclassification of cannabis from C to B. There has also been recent and telling criticism of the 1971 Act because it contains no mention of alcohol or tobacco[5] – both drugs taken for pleasure which kill many tens of times more users than illegal drugs.

Of all the illegal drugs heroin and other opiates stand alone, not because their use is necessarily more hazardous than others, but because they are so fiercely addictive, and once acquired the habit needs feeding two or three times a day to avoid the awful symptoms of withdrawal. Other drugs such as cocaine, cannabis, amphetamines, LSD, ketamine, ecstasy, tranquilizers and solvents can be addictive, but usually are not. They are usually taken in certain social or other circumstances, rather like alcohol. This is known as recreational use, which generally causes little harm to health or social functioning. This is not to say that any narcotic drug is safe and without any potential trouble. All currently illegal drugs can cause harm to health, particularly if they are taken in combination with other drugs or alcohol. The route by which a drug is taken is also important.

Injection into a vein always increases the risks, the most important of which is an overdose, which can be lethal. Ecstasy tablets, many thousands of which are consumed every weekend, have been responsible for a number of well-publicized deaths. Acquiring a drug habit is hazardous and expensive, it exposes the user to the risk of arrest, and some drugs, most notably heroin, have the capacity to ruin lives even if they are not particularly harmful to health. The problem arises when use becomes immoderate, or when cocktails of several drugs, often mixed with alcohol, are consumed. Such users are a danger to themselves and to society. It is no surprise that so many people wish to see all such drugs removed from the social scene.

Drugs are now a commanding problem throughout the world, sustained by the legions of people who take them, and indeed, if no one was interested in taking them they would do no harm and disappear. All illegal drugs, as well as alcohol and tobacco, are used because, in various ways, they affect the way we feel – they give us pleasure. But the majority of us do not want to take illegal drugs, though many will know and value the effect of alcohol or tobacco. Why should this be? It is partly a matter of personal taste, just as is the decision to smoke a cigarette or not. We all have different needs and ways of coping with our emotions. And, we have different personalities and ways of thinking and behaving. Some are adventurous and like taking risks, while others are timid and risk-averse. The adventurous risk-takers will do things that others will not, and taking pills when offered may be one of them. And if they are illegal, for many, they will be more attractive. And there may be social pressures at play, such as encouragement by an older and admired friend.

Thus it is that some people will experiment and perhaps persist in taking a drug which others will refuse. If the experimentation continues it may become a habit because pleasure is powerfully reinforcing. If the drug happens to be an opiate there will come a time when it has to be taken every day – dependence has arrived and addiction looms.

It is common to talk about a person having an addictive personality. The proposition is that such people are different from others, and that they will fall into a pattern of addictive behaviour, which might be genetically determined. Reality proves to be more complicated. There is no simple genetic explanation for addictive behaviour, though genetic make-up will have some influence. It is perhaps best to talk of such people as general risk-takers, whose experimentation leads on to other things. Whatever the ultimate explanation, some people become addicted to one or more drugs, others to chocolate, and yet others to gambling or shopping, or to other compulsive behaviours.

There are stages on the road to addiction. Habituation implies that you have a habit of taking a particular drug, but that it is still possible to stop without unpleasantness. Dependency means that it will be unpleasant to stop, but still possible. Addiction implies that you have a habit that must be fed to avoid the awful symptoms of withdrawal. It consumes your life. It is a powerful state of mind and body. It is an obsession that reduces normal and sensible people to slavery. The cravings dominate life and control behaviour, and satisfying them becomes the only purpose of existence. They are the torment against which the addict must find the strength to struggle, and they leave him no peace. Addiction is a compulsion to which surrender is inevitable.

Heroin is a brainwasher, which bends reason. It behaves like a computer virus with a predilection for the human brain, which it re-programmes to reject and pervert thoughts of living an abstinent life. Even addicts approaching middle life, who are stable on an opiate substitute and have not touched heroin for years, who want to get clean, have an incomprehensible reluctance to take the steps they know to be necessary and entirely in their own interests. Heroin has a power which is unique.

The World Health Organization defines addiction as 'a state, psychic and sometimes physical, resulting from the interaction between a living organism and a drug, characterized by behavioural and other responses that always include a compulsion to take the drug on a continuous or periodic basis in order to experience its psychic effects, and sometimes to avoid the discomfort of its absence. Tolerance may or may not be present. A person may be dependent on more than one drug.'

The heroin high or 'buzz' is difficult to describe, for it is a very personal and private experience. It has different aspects and intensities, which reflect, in part, the route of administration. The calmer, more peaceful state induced by smoking heroin is captured in one description: 'somewhere deep down in your centre there's a glow, a throb, a tingle. A golden thread runs up your spine and out through the top of your head. A happy smack puppet, warm and comfortable, your body dangles around this taut, buzzing chord. You are stoned.'[6]

This vision of a controlled and serene world is in stark contrast to the overwhelming and brutal description of the first experience of an intravenous injection of heroin, by the same author: 'It's like waiting for a distant thunderstorm to move overhead. A strange foreboding. A bizarre awesome calm. It's in your blood, moving towards your brain, relentlessly, unstoppable and inevitable. A feeling starts to grow like a rumble from the horizon. The feeling swells, surging, soaring, crashing, screaming to a devastating crescendo. The gear smashes against the top of your skull with the power of an uncapped oil well. You won't be able to bear the intense ecstasy. It is all too much. Your body may fall apart. The rock that is your head shatters harmlessly into a million sparkling, tinkling smithereens. They tumble at a thousand miles an hour straight back down over your body, warming, insulating, tingling, denying all pain, fear and sadness. You are stoned, you are high. You are above and below reality and law.'[7]

Most people must wonder why their less wise colleagues indulge in behaviour which carries the risk that they may become addicted. Could it possibly be worth it? The answer is a resounding 'yes', but then the qualifications start. Anyone with a newly acquired opiate habit enters an extraordinary world. It is one of relaxation, contentment and peace, where anxiety and worry have no place. It is a world in which your mental capacities seem to become enhanced, and the breadth of your thoughts expand. Your self-confidence soars. It is like entering a hall of mirrors which reflect back at you a series of images ever more noble, more handsome, more confident and more secure. It is heaven on earth, the paradise of which we dream, from which all woes and cares are ruthlessly excluded. But its lustre dims and fades, and the real world creeps back like the dawn, as hours pass. The terrible reality must then be faced that unless you take some more heroin you will have to endure the misery of withdrawal.

This Nirvana can only be visited with a time-expiry ticket. This wondrous phase of addiction does not last. In weeks or months it gradually loses its perfection. The buzz begins to fade, and many will have to increase their dose even to glimpse the world they recently inhabited with such sublime contentment. Addiction has been described by one heroin user as 'a form of mourning for the irrecoverable glories of the first time'.[8] Some addicts get so desperate to recapture these early experiences that they will abandon heroin and lead an abstinent life for a time to allow their brain receptors to regain their sensitivity. They can then take up their habit again, and, for a short time, re-enter the world they yearn for. It is a powerful testimony to the attraction of the opiate world.

The next phase is the long hard slog, which is firmly rooted in the real world, and offers little magic. For most, the buzz has gone, and the reason for using opiates is to avoid withdrawal. A few can recapture some reminder of the past, particularly if they inject intravenously, but most have ruefully to admit that their habit, with all its dangers, miseries, and costs, now serves no purpose other than to stop them feeling unwell. But even at this stage it does not really occur to many that the nightmare could be over if they abandon their habit and get clean. Addicts are conditioned to believe that to do so would be more painful and difficult than they could bear. Throwing away the crutches that have supported their lives is a big and dangerous adventure. Furthermore, the issues and problems from which they sought escape may yet be unresolved. Nevertheless, many addicts do start to think more rationally about their lives, and so take purposeful steps towards abstention. It often starts when they get some inkling of the extremities to which drugs have led them, and the idea of drugs begins to lose its lustre.

Once the second phase of addiction is well-established, with the glory fading and the habit yielding diminishing returns, many addicts will have started to look seriously for some help. They will have the hope and intention of detoxifying, and leading a normal abstinent life. For many it does not work out like that. It may be that treatment is too demanding, or is inadequate to stop them supplementing with street drugs. More often it is that heroin continues to hold too strong an attraction for them. Or it may be that they are unable to find a new and satisfying purpose to fill the gap in their lives that would be left by the passing of opiates. There are many reasons for failing to get clean, and for failing to stay clean, but the commonest is that heroin is just too nice to give up. A minority of users will take the conscious decision to remain on an opiate substitute prescription for the foreseeable future, which often means the rest of their lives. For some couples, taking drugs together is a ceremony which they enjoy and value – for them it takes the place of having a drink together. Others try to persuade themselves that they will get clean 'one day', but in reality that day never dawns. They know deep down that they will continue until the end.

All these people enter the third phase of opium use – sometimes called end-stage addiction. They get no pleasure in the old sense from their habit, but it is companionable, and they retain their senior membership of the tribe of drug takers. In most cases they will not have touched heroin for many years, and have no thoughts of ever doing so. They will be living quite normal lives in full-time work or retirement, and drugs – albeit prescribed opiates – are their indulgence and recreation. Some of them will be nursing the enduring legacy of the more heady days of their careers as drug users. Many live with the consequences of Hepatitis C, or have had to be treated for them. A few will be HIV positive, and live with the threat of AIDS. The fever and chaos, the agony and ecstasy of their younger days, are replaced by peaceful resignation, tinged with regrets for what might have been.

The large majority of addicts, however, do give up drugs. It is one of the many myths surrounding the subject of drugs that addicts are forever cast into outer darkness. A few die from self-administered overdoses if they are injectors, and a few continue to take an opiate substitute in a safe and controlled way. The rest just stop using, usually between the ages of thirty-five and forty-five, and become normal, working, tax-paying citizens. They do it because drugs are no longer very interesting. It often coincides with a newly found sense of maturity and of having 'grown up'. But they will sometimes struggle to make up for the experiences of youth, which were denied to them because they were stolen by heroin. Recreational users of the less addictive drugs usually lose their taste for them as their lives change, and as the party scene loses its attractions.

As if to bear witness to all this, there are plenty of ageing rock stars still in the public eye. In most cases they have been clean for years, but their early adult years were spent pickled in drugs. The past has taken some kind of a toll, and many of them have high-mileage faces, but there are still large audiences for their music.

Views about the nature of addiction have changed over the years. There have been many. It was 'a bad habit of the morally weak', 'moral bankruptcy', a product of 'diseased cravings and paralysed control', and the result 'of abnormal brain structure'. Attention has focused more recently on how it should be managed rather than on conjectures about its cause, which remains an enigma. It is now regarded, at least in Britain, as largely a medical and public health problem, though it is also subject to the law, which remains distinctly prohibitionist. This remains an awkward relationship, for the law and medicine are uneasy bedfellows. Every now and again new research seems to point to some brain abnormality in addicts, and the possibility that addiction is a real brain disease,[9] but on present evidence that possibility cannot be sustained.

An understanding of the nature and features of addiction is important to any debate about the direction of drug policy in the future. Most of us have never been under the extreme degree of compulsion and obsession, which are universal features of addiction. We simply do not know, nor can we imagine, what it feels like. To most it is an extreme and incomprehensible behaviour. Nevertheless, it has to be taken seriously because it never responds to exhortations to 'pull yourself together and snap out of it.' To even think that it might is totally to misunderstand the nature of addiction.

There is another issue that we must take account of. The use of mind-altering substances has been a constant and deeply rooted appetite throughout human history. It is an instinctive behaviour, and, as such, must be regarded as normal. Smoking and sensible drinking have always been accepted as normal habits. But a problem arises when someone chooses to use something different –

illegal drugs – to achieve the same effect. That is regarded as abnormal behaviour. The *intoxicant*, not the intoxication, becomes the problem. But satisfying a normal human need is a good and necessary thing to do, so one might suppose that anything which can achieve this is also good and necessary. But this is not the case.

Only tobacco and alcohol have society's seal of approval, though they kill a hundred times more of their users than other substances having the same effect, which society regards as illegal. Intoxication, whether by alcohol, music or a deeply affecting experience, is an integral, normal and positive adjunct to the human condition. It is only deemed bad and abnormal when induced by other agents, those which we call illegal drugs. And there is a further question we must ask. If the most successful species the planet has ever known has this innate need, it is highly likely that it serves some positive and useful purpose, provided, of course, that it is indulged reasonably.

Most would agree that an altered state of mind allows the imagination to soar, although often the insights obtained are not as brilliant and important in the sober light of day as they seemed at the time. Alcohol and psycho-active plants have played a part in religious ceremony for millennia, and intoxicants are also a social cohesive. But the clearest benefit of occasional intoxication is the re-creation of the human spirit, and the renewal of the soul, which it so often brings. In this respect drug use can be seen as a change agent in society. It is possible that there is another purpose not yet discovered, but it is perverse to insist that it can only be accessed with alcohol as the one key, when all the keys in the bunch fit the lock.

This is not being advanced as an argument that we *need* illegal mind-altering drugs. After all, the great majority of the world's population have never used an illegal drug, but the number of people who do not consume some alcohol or smoke tobacco is an order of magnitude fewer. These two substances between them satisfy the requirements of almost everybody who has the sporadic need to feel a little different for a short time, which is most of the world's population. And they are both legal practically everywhere in the world, even if custom or religion dictates that one or the other should not be used, or personal taste means you choose not to. But to deny the existence of this instinctive feeling would not serve the purposes of a fair debate.

Recent figures suggest that there are about 327,000 'problem drug users' in England and Wales[10] – defined as users of heroin and/or crack cocaine – as well as 10-15 million occasional or recreational users of other illegal drugs.[11] Heroin can be delivered to your door in most parts of the country faster than an emergency ambulance. Recreational drug use has become a normal part of the lives of the great majority of young people. This is an issue of absolutely crucial importance to those responsible for making drug policy. Unless they understand the extent and depth to which drugs have penetrated our society today, they have no chance of formulating a policy which will be relevant, and have any chance at all of being effective. Ask any young person about drugs and you will get an answer somewhere between 'all my friends take drugs' and, 'I know lots of people who do, but I'm not interested.' Numbers of drug takers are discussed elsewhere in this book, but statistics have little personal impact. Indirect evidence suggests that illegal drug use is even more widespread than many of the estimates. For example, an Italian group of investigators have repeated the work they first did analysing the breakdown of cocaine products in the waters of the River Po below Milan. Their findings in the River Thames are similar,[12] and indicate that up to eight times more cocaine is used in London every day than official estimates suggest.

Evidence of drug taking crops up in unexpected places: traces of cocaine have been found in swabs taken from lavatories and bars in the House of Commons, and from a lavatory in the House of Lords.[13] Forty-one of forty-six swabs taken in the European Parliament buildings in Brussels were positive for cocaine.[14] A satirical television programme interviewed Italian Deputies about the 2007 budget outside the parliament buildings in Rome. They were eager to give their views and welcomed the opportunity of media exposure. A make-up girl then swabbed their sweating brows, and the swabs were analysed for drugs. Of the fifty interviewed, sixteen proved positive, twelve for cannabis and four for cocaine.[15] The final irony was that when the story leaked out the programme was withdrawn and never broadcast. The television station was owned by Silvio Berlusconi.

Irrespective of the stories above, drug taking is overwhelmingly a habit of the young. Drug policy is formulated and written by civil servants over the age of forty, who are most unlikely to be drug takers, and almost certainly have no understanding of the magnitude of the problem they are addressing. The issue that arises is whether or not it is possible to eradicate drugs from our society. It is a subject to which we will return later in this book, for it has, or should have, a profound influence on the development of policy.

In spite of all the initiatives and the expenditure of a very serious amount of public money, illegal drugs are today the most efficiently distributed commodity in the country, and are bought and used by many millions of people who do not believe that they are transgressing any principle of natural justice. That is the massive challenge which public policy and public money have today almost totally failed to change.

2 Attempting to Address the Problem

In 1898 the United States of America annexed the Philippines at the end of the Spanish-American war. The new American masters were horrified by what they found. The opium dens of Manila and elsewhere were patronized by the Chinese, while access was forbidden to the Filipinos, to whom it was also illegal to sell opium. Opium dens had been very successfully operated by the former Spanish colonial rulers by selling concessions to the highest bidder, who always proved to be Chinese. It was a very profitable arrangement for all concerned. The new administration declared that such a discriminatory monopoly was contrary to American theories of government, the consequence of which was a considerable increase in opium consumption, particularly by the Filipinos. The Governor, William Taft, was persuaded that the former system, a pragmatic and effective arrangement for control widespread in the Far East at the time, should be restored. The American missionaries, headed by the Canadian Methodist Bishop of Manila, Charles Henry Brent, mounted a stern campaign of resistance on moral grounds, and the proposal was withdrawn in 1902. Instead, opium use and sale was prohibited outright. This was a heaven-sent opportunity for the Chinese underworld to provide illegally for the needs of opium users, both Chinese and Filipino, and the new Manila government was no match for them.

This was not the first occasion on which American officialdom had come into contact with opium dens. In 1875, San Francisco passed a city ordinance forbidding young whites to patronize the opium dens serving the needs of the Chinese population, which had arrived from Hong Kong and the mainland to work in building the railways and in the gold mines of California. Over the next fifteen years or so several other cities followed San Francisco's example. These measures, however, had the effect of criminalizing the users, rather than in any way controlling the supply of drugs.

Bishop Brent of Manila was an effective and persuasive anti-drug campaigner, who cajoled President Theodore Roosevelt into convening the 1909 Opium Commission in Shanghai. At the same time the US government passed the Smoking Opium Exclusion Act, the purpose of which was to raise the moral tone of the American contribution at the Shanghai meeting. Its effect, however, was very different. Opium became more difficult to obtain, and hence more expensive. This in turn resulted in diverting users away from smoking opium to using cheaper heroin, increasing its use greatly as a result. Already we are able to see how ill-considered measures, passed by those who do not understand the problems, have damaging or counter-productive consequences. It is a theme that we will see repeatedly in this book.

Three years after the Shanghai Commission, the first international attempt at narcotics control took place in The Hague. The 1912 Hague Convention, chaired by Bishop Brent, resulted in the International Opium Convention, signed by twelve nations. This must be considered as the origin of the criminalization of drugs on the world stage, which today we call prohibition. It set out to achieve the 'general suppression' of opium, morphine and cocaine abuse by ensuring that they were made only for 'medical and legitimate purposes'. Signatory nations were also required to introduce legislation making possession of these drugs a penal offence.

Meanwhile in America, most states passed laws controlling the availability of opiates and cocaine, and in a few cases, of marijuana. In 1906, the Pure Food and Drugs Act attempted, not altogether successfully, to control their labelling and sale. And, in 1914, the Harrison Act regulated the distribution, prescription, taxation and sale of all opiate and cocaine-containing preparations, which henceforward required a doctor's prescription. It was a sensible bit of legislation, which stood the test of time.

In 1924, the League of Nations convened another Opium Conference in Geneva. The US delegation walked out of negotiations because they were not sufficiently prohibitionist. Ultimately, and after much argument and time, the Conference ensured that amounts of opiates only legitimately required could be manufactured in Europe. Meanwhile, in 1923, the US had been unable to persuade Turkey to introduce crops to substitute for opium poppies, and that country went on to become one of the most important producers in the world. But gradually, by the late 1930s and under inexorable pressure from America, legal overproduction ceased, immediately replaced by illicit, clandestine and criminal supplies. Once again, well-meaning but ignorant policies had handed a whole industry to international criminal gangs, and they could not believe their luck.

All the while, the United States was building and consolidating its prohibitionist credentials. In 1919, the Supreme Court issued a judgement that doctors were not to prescribe opiates for maintenance purposes. This was followed in 1922 by another Supreme Court ruling that doctors were not to prescribe opiates, even in diminishing quantities, as part of an addict's withdrawal treatment. In the same year, the Jones-Miller Act prohibited importation of heroin, and two years later, in 1924, the Porter Act brought an end to the manufacture and medical use of heroin altogether in the US – an Act that is still in force today. The consequences of all this draconian legislation were disastrous. And, of course, predictable. Thousands of addicts found themselves without any legal source of opiates, and were thus driven to seek illegal supplies. So bad was the situation that a few municipal authorities set up dispensaries for these unfortunates, rather than allow them to be forced into illegal dealings. They, and the doctors working with them, were persecuted and intimidated by the Narcotics Division of the Prohibition Unit.

Many addicts, predictably, became small-time dealers to protect their supplies, and sold small amounts to the young and impressionable, so spreading the contagion and exacerbating the problem. The prisons started to fill up. More and more states enacted prohibition of the possession of opiates, cocaine, and even of a hypodermic syringe. Possession of one of these drugs without a prescription was held to be presumptive evidence of illegal importation, which thus made possession a federal crime. Indeed addiction itself became, in effect, a crime at a time when increasing numbers of doctors were coming to regard it as a medical condition. Rigidly enforced prohibition, with no legal source of drugs whatever, even for treatment, was an ideal environment in which drug trafficking gangsters could thrive. To them, laws prohibiting manufacture and importation of drugs were manna from heaven.

Marijuana did not escape the zeal of the prohibitionists. Smoking marijuana was endemic in Mexico, and the large numbers of Mexican migrant workers brought it with them. Its use in the US was given a tremendous boost by the prohibition of alcohol in 1920, which spawned 'tea-pads', providing marijuana, alongside the 'speak-easies' selling bootleg liquor. West Indian marijuana also started to come into the Gulf ports, and until overtaken by legislation, was sold in chemist's shops in the South. Mexican users were poor, ill-educated and disenfranchised, and they were mercilessly, and often illegally, persecuted by prohibitionist law-enforcers. In 1937, marijuana was outlawed in every state, and the Federal government passed the Marijuana Tax Bill. This was a shocking piece of legislation, passed by the House of Representatives in half an hour, without any medical or scientific evidence, by politicians who knew nothing about marijuana, or what effects it had.

It is reasonable to wonder what forces moulded all these counter-productive and ill-considered legal measures. Firstly, they enjoyed wide support from ordinary law-abiding but ignorant citizens, who trusted their politicians to do the right thing. Secondly, there was a consistent and well-orchestrated campaign to demonize drugs and their users, and so to confirm the prejudices of the moral majority. This derived from genuine feelings of horror many Americans had towards opium and marijuana smoking in other cultures of which they had no knowledge or interest in. Thirdly, the excesses of the Temperance Movement were fresh in some minds, though one might have reflected on the less positive consequences of its white-hot zeal. And lastly, there were figures of supposed authority who made wildly exaggerated or unfounded statements about the evils of drugs to further their own personal or political purposes.

During the Second World War, drug taking in the US diminished greatly. As we have seen, there were no legal sources of supply, and the criminal gangs of traffickers were otherwise occupied. When the war was over, however, they were back in business. The US heroin market was taken over by the Cosa Nostra, led by 'Lucky' Luciano and Meyer Lansky. Luciano was let out of prison, where he was serving a long sentence for numerous racketeering charges, in recognition of favours rendered to US naval and military intelligence during the war. He was deported to Italy, where he took over the local Mafia and built up a highly successful and profitable heroin trafficking organization, culminating in the 'French Connection'. This processed-morphine base in Marseilles, for a time, supplied 95 per cent of all the heroin entering America. By 1952 there were three times more heroin addicts in the US than there had been before the war.

Harry Anslinger had been appointed Commissioner of the Federal Bureau of Narcotics in 1930. He was able, fiercely ambitious, and Andrew Mellon's son-in-law. He used exaggeration and lies to great effect both with politicians and the press, and was largely responsible for Congress passing the Boggs Act in 1951. This required judges to impose prison sentences of two, five and ten years on first, second and third convictions for possession of any narcotic drug, with no parole for second and subsequent offences. Five years later, the even more draconian Narcotic Control Act increased sentences to 10, 20 and 40 years for possession of marijuana, and up to 40 years for subsequent convictions. Selling to a minor got a minimum of 10 years, and a possible life sentence or even the death penalty, on the recommendation of a jury. In 1970, a measure of sanity returned when Congress repealed mandatory sentencing for marijuana offences.

In 1966, Nelson Rockefeller decided that he would make tough anti-drug laws the corner-stone of his campaign to become Governor of New York State. He won, and the notorious Rockefeller drug laws were passed in 1973. A mandatory sentence of 15 years to life was to be given to all who were convicted of possessing or selling two ounces (56 grams) or more of any narcotic drug, including marijuana, LSD and amphetamines. These laws represent the apogee of attempts to punish drug users into submission. They proved to be unworkable and had no effect on crime rates. Subsequently, they were somewhat watered down, as public support for tough sentences for marijuana use, which was by then widespread, had begun to waver. Several states decriminalized marijuana for personal use, and this general trend has continued.

In 1968, Richard Nixon won the Republican nomination for President, and he set about choosing the issues he hoped his administration would be remembered for. There were a number of candidates: a successful conclusion to the war in Vietnam; continued and uncompromising opposition to communism throughout the world; the championing of human rights on the international stage; or embracing expansionist economic policies to make all Americans better off. He chose none of these, taking his inspiration from Nelson Rockefeller. On 17 June 1971, in a nationwide television address, he declared his 'War on Drugs'. To rely on notable achievements in human rights might well backfire, especially as America itself was at war – the war in Vietnam was bogged down and not going well for America, and was losing public support; his anti-communist credentials were waning; the economy was too difficult and risky.

What Nixon needed was a war which he could win – or at least one which he thought he could win. His political allies who had supported the war in Vietnam were seeing their popularity slump. When he announced his 'all-out offensive' against drugs they rallied to his cause, and voted plenty of money. Drugs, Nixon said, were the first domestic concern of the day, heroin users were responsible for two billion dollars worth of property crime every year, and it was his opinion that drugs would destroy America. There were some less public reasons why Nixon espoused this cause. He loathed the hippies, whom he regarded as hedonists and un-American, as well as drug takers, and he felt that they needed to e brought to heel and punished for their obvious enjoyment of life. He was also, and very understandably, alarmed by the use of heroin by young GIs in Vietnam. Evidently it did not occur to him that to send eighteen-year olds to fight a war in which they did not believe, without access to alcohol, might cause problems. The US military would only allow alcohol to be sold to those over twenty-one – the young GIs were old enough to die for their country, but could not be trusted with a few beers. It was not surprising that some should seek solace from the pressures of war with a smoke of heroin.

For the first two years the anti-drug programme, directed by Dr Jerome Jaffe, went well. But it did not last. It was not to be long before Nixon took further action that had catastrophic consequences for the United States of America, as we shall see in Chapter 3. When Mexico refused to allow the US to destroy its poppy and marijuana crops by aerial spraying, Nixon responded by closing the US-Mexican border. Hundreds of thousands who had reason to cross the border were searched, while public opinion approved vocally of this 'tough' action. In the long term there were deeply damaging consequences for the US. With hindsight it is easy to say that this was all predictable. At the time, it seems that nobody thought about it. Nevertheless, Nixon pressed on ruthlessly. He tried to persuade producers in Turkey, Mexico and the Golden Triangle in South East Asia to eradicate poppy growing, with only modest success – Turkey did suppress growth in exchange for $20 million.

Meanwhile, the President must have known that CIA involvement in South East Asia came at a price. The war against communism was fought by proxy armies which grew and traded in heroin, and it was done with the connivance, and even the active assistance of the Americans. Much of what they helped to produce and transport found its way onto the streets of America. Importantly, Nixon reorganized government anti-drug agencies without proper Congressional approval. The new Bureau of Narcotics and Dangerous Drugs was able to operate anywhere in the world, and effectively to function outside the law.

The year 1976 saw an interesting and important legal decision handed down. Robert Randall was a young man with glaucoma, which was threatening his eyesight. He had found that smoking several marijuana joints a day stopped progression of the disease, whereas all the conventional treatments did not. He was arrested for growing marijuana for his own use, and fought a remarkably persistent legal campaign. He won his case, and the US government was forced to supply him with legal marijuana cigarettes, for which purpose they had to grow it on a US Federal farm. However, in due course, the US Supreme Court ruled that this was illegal, and that the use of marijuana was not legal for medicinal purposes.

The Ford and Carter administrations continued to wage 'War on Drugs', but with diminished zeal. President Carter went so far as to advocate decriminalization of marijuana on the very reasonable grounds that 'penalties against possession of a drug should not be more damaging to an individual than the use of the drug itself', but he was unable to prevail on Congress to take action. There were even rumours that Hamilton Jordan, Carter's White House Chief of Staff, enjoyed an occasional joint. During these relatively relaxed years eleven states effectively decriminalized marijuana use, with no discernable rise in its use.

In 1979, the Carter administration started to supply arms to the Mujahedin guerrillas in Afghanistan, who were fighting the Russian invaders. Within a very short time Afghanistan overtook

Burma as the largest supplier of illegal opium in the world, which was processed in laboratories in the south of the country, and across the border in the wild tribal areas of Pakistan. Cheap Afghan heroin had started to increase the numbers of heroin addicts in America, and attitudes began to harden. The government responded by enlarging the Drug Enforcement Administration, which already was able to operate outside America.

By 1982, President Reagan had re-launched the hard-line 'War on Drugs'. However, events were unfolding which temporarily moved the administration's concerns away from the domestic drug scene. The trafficking of cocaine and heroin from South America became an even bigger problem. President Reagan became mired in the Iran-Contra affair, which generated funds to support the anti-communist Contra forces in Nicaragua, but at the price of increasing involvement of the CIA in cynical and illegal activities. The increased powers granted to the CIA and other federal anti-drug agencies meant that they became much less accountable, and were responsible for incidents in which they abused their power and acted illegally.

By 1983, crack cocaine had become widely available in the cities and ghettos of America. This was a form of cocaine that could be smoked, and so reach the brain and exert its effect in seconds. Cocaine deaths started to rise, and 1986 it was estimated that 5,000 Americans tried the drug for the first time every day. One in eleven of the population admitted to its recreational use at some time. Urine testing became commonplace at work. Crime soared, gangs of suppliers fought each other on the streets, numbers of users rose and the purity of street drugs rose while their price fell. Reagan responded by spending more and more on futile attempts to prevent drugs coming into the country. He passed the Anti-Drug Abuse Act in 1986, which called for prison sentences for drug dealers operating near schools. It also provided for a mandatory sentence of five years in prison for possession of five grams of crack – one hundred times more punitive than that for possession of the same quantity of powdered cocaine.

At the same time his wife, Nancy Reagan, launched her anti-drug campaign under the slogan 'Just say no'. In January 1981, at the time of her arrival at the White House, she had raised over $1 million to do up the private apartments, and to buy new china for formal banquets. All this, at a time of rising unemployment, brought her withering criticism in the press. There was a need to reinvent herself, which she did very successfully by espousing the anti-drug cause. But she also unwisely endorsed several right wing organizations, like Straight Inc., which was later unmasked as a criminal concern. She also became involved with the Parents' Resource Institute for Drug Education (PRIDE), a fanatical and idealistic, but well-meaning organization. Her efforts were undoubtedly sincere, but also naive. While she did have a marginal effect in reducing drug use among adolescents for a time, almost certainly among those who were in any case equivocal about drugs, she demonstrated an almost stupefying lack of insight and ignorance of the motives and intentions of most drug takers.

In 1987, official US government reports began to criticize drug policy for being 'diffuse and overlapping.' Distinguished voices, like Milton Friedman and William Buckley, started to be raised in dissent at current policy. In spite of its conspicuous failure, the new President, George Bush Sr, renewed the pledge to continue the 'War', driven by public opinion, which wanted ever-tougher action on drugs and crime. His strategy was to increase the role of the military, and to spend more money on more federal agents, and more judges and prosecutors. There was no lack of enthusiasm for applying the existing anti-drug laws, and there was a huge new prison-building programme to accommodate the hundreds of thousands of non-violent drug users who were being deprived of their freedom.

US Special Forces were even prepared to go after and arrest traffickers anywhere in the world, without the agreement of the country concerned. By the end of the 1990s, the increasing militarization of the 'War on Drugs' was welcomed by the Pentagon, which, with the fall of communism, was facing major budget cuts.

By the time of the 1992 presidential election it was clear that drugs could not be kept out of the country. President Clinton promised to put more effort into addiction treatment and prevention. It might have been reasonable to anticipate that the Democrat Clinton would have presided over some softening of drug policy. It was not to be, though his style was distinctly more muted than his predecessors. During the election campaign it emerged that he had smoked cannabis when he was at Oxford, but that he 'did not inhale'. This admission became a serious threat to his campaign. Perhaps it was a desire to repair his anti-drug credentials which did not allow a policy rethink, and he was certainly under constant pressure from the drug warriors in Congress.

The existing juggernaut rolled on without a pause. Police powers increased, new prisons were built, and the total prison population rose from 1.3 million to over 2 million during Clinton's presidency. Now the US has the highest imprisonment rate in the world – five times more citizens being incarcerated per head of population than is the case in Britain. The huge increase in recent years consists of those convicted of drug offences, the great majority of whom are non-violent. Yet evidence that deprivation of liberty is effective in changing drug-related behaviour is lacking, while there is a strong suggestion that violence is learned in prison, and that the social and family consequences of detention are incalculable.

The 1984 Omnibus Crime Bill had allowed agencies seizing the assets of criminals to sell them, and to keep the proceeds for their own use. Children attending drug education sessions run by the police were invited to give the names of any drug users they knew, even their parents. Clinton's Surgeon General, Dr Joycelyn Elders, proved to be an embarrassment because she was sympathetic to the medicinal use of marijuana, and in spite of legislation in many states in favour, it was vetoed by Clinton. Perhaps the issue which most epitomized the intransigence of Clinton's drug policy was his refusal to support the roll-out of needle exchanges.

Federally funded research had proved that these reduced the incidence of AIDS and Hepatitis C, but their continued roll-out was never sanctioned '[because] it would send the wrong message to our young people'. This was a triumph for moral bigotry over compassion, for which many will have already paid with their lives. Instead, Clinton issued the mandatory warning about tough action, and continued economic and military aid for producer countries. It is an irony that today one of the main causes espoused by the William J Clinton Charitable Foundation is the worldwide campaign against HIV/AIDS.

President Bush Junior was by inclination a drug warrior, but his credentials were dented by strong rumours that he had taken cocaine and marijuana in his youth. He certainly had a conviction for driving under the influence of alcohol. He pursued rigidly prohibitionist policies, and frustrated research efforts, by all means in his power, to define the role of marijuana in medicine.

New thinking is now evident and taking practical effect. The use of marijuana for medicinal purposes, such as the alleviation of chemotherapy-induced nausea or glaucoma, is now legal in thirteen states, and at least as many will consider a similar course in the near future. However, this concession is being widely abused, and there are plenty of doctors who will provide the necessary certificate on the most dubious medical grounds, and for the payment of $100. Los Angeles how has over one hundred 'dispensaries'.

There are, too, a few hints that government policy might be changing. The Obama administration was seen to be tip-toeing away from the excesses of the 'War on Drugs', the very name of which is quietly being dropped. The presidents of South American drug-producing countries are tired of being lectured by the United States, and are now pointing out that the ghastly toll of drug-related murders, particularly in Mexico, is abetted by the flood of American guns pouring across the border, and that none of these problems would exist if the United States did not have such a great appetite for cocaine. At the time of writing there seems a real possibility that the US might reconsider its drug policy – nothing could be as ill-considered and counter-productive as the present situation.

It can be argued that American drug policy is a matter for America alone, yet it is vital to the success f this radical reform of policy that it operates internationally by multi-lateral agreement between the countries of the world. Drugs respect no boundaries.

One of the underlying principles of US drug policy has been a legitimate concern for all nations. America is an exceptionally powerful nation, which is not reticent in seeking to impose its will on others, and to this end it is prepared to exert coercive pressure until it succeeds. Its tone is often hectoring. Because the United States did not like some of the conclusions of the largest and most sophisticated study of cocaine ever undertaken, it suppressed the report by the World Health Organization by threatening to withdraw all financial and other support. The US government took the view that the report's findings were directly, and clearly inconveniently, contrary to the spurious 'facts' which underpinned the 'War on Drugs'. The report was leaked and published on the internet.[16] Every nation shares America's revulsion with illegal drugs, and the misery and mayhem they bring in their wake, but few continue to share America's conviction that their policies are the most effective remedies. This being the case, we have a right to take issue with aspects of policy, and to pursue alternative options.

In Britain, policy on drugs began with the signing in 1912 of The Hague International Opium Convention. The British government dragged its feet because difficulties arose in the interpretation of 'medical and legitimate purposes'. This was significant because it was all too obvious that, although there were not many addicts, they would seek illegal supplies unless workable arrangements were in place for them. This was a welcome glimpse of common sense, which sometimes, but not always, has informed the development of drug policy in Britain.

The eventual outcomes were The Dangerous Drugs Act of 1920 and the Dangerous Drugs Regulations of 1921, which gave legal force to The Hague Convention recommendations. But the ambiguities and uncertainties of what constituted legitimate use of opiates and cocaine persisted – in particular the question of prescribing for addicts.

Clearly some doctors took an extreme view of what use was proper, and there were several cases where doctors had themselves become addicted to opiates, and prescribed generously for themselves. This led, in 1924, to a blacklist of doctors and addicted patients, compiled by the Home Office, but the policy of prescribing for addicts was professionally controversial and practically problematic. In 1923, a Ministry of Health report had concluded that sudden withdrawal of an addict's drugs was impossible unless done in hospital, and that addiction was a disease. The uncertainty rumbled on. It was time for an authoritative lead.

The Ministry of Health set up a committee under the chairmanship of Sir Humphrey Rolleston, the then President of the Royal College of Physicians. It reported in 1926 that it was legitimate to prescribe heroin and morphine in gradually reducing doses for addicts undergoing treatment.[17] It was also acceptable for addicts who were unable to give up opiates, because either their withdrawal symptoms were unmanageable, or because they were unable to function in society without some opiate maintenance. This report was of signal importance, for it confirmed that, in Britain at least, addiction and its treatment was a medical problem, and that, provided it complied with the prescribing regulations, it was not a concern for the police. It was a humane and common sense report.

It was, nevertheless, necessary to put in place a number of structures to ensure compliance with legislation, and with the spirit of the Rolleston Report. The most notable were the Home Office Drugs Inspectorate; the periodic review of pharmacy records by the police, and the setting up of a register of addicts by the Home Office. In 1931, there were 245 on the register. There soon followed mechanisms for dealing with addicted doctors, and those who prescribed for addicts without any attempt to treat them.

Throughout the 1930s and the Second World War there was little legislation and the number of addicts remained very small and stable. They were, in the main, therapeutic addicts whose dependence was due to prolonged treatment with opiates for pain, or professionals who had access to drugs, such as doctors, nurses, veterinary surgeons or pharmacists. They obtained their prescriptions from doctors willing to look after them.

After the War, however, things changed radically. It started with quantities of cannabis introduced by West Indian immigrants, turning up in clubs and being bought by local users. A black market in heroin also soon became established, initially fuelled by existing addicts selling off part of their over-generous prescriptions from the handful of doctors who were known to be a soft touch, and benefitting financially by prescribing. The supply was soon augmented by thefts from hospitals and chemists' shops.

In 1955, there was a curious and undignified attempt to ban the production of medicinal heroin altogether. Since the 1930s, there had been a number of attempts by international bodies to do this, and some countries had complied. Rather improbably, the British government announced that when the licences expired under which therapeutic heroin was produced, they would not be renewed. Somewhat slowly, the medical profession, individually and collectively, mobilized their opposition, and a year later the policy was reversed. It was a strange episode – the government and the medical profession had sleep-walked into a wrong and illogical decision before the British Medical Association woke up.

In 1958, the first Brain Committee was set up under the chairmanship of Sir Russell Brain, a past President of the Royal College of Physicians. It was a response to international moves to ban legitimate heroin manufacture, and to the advent of some new synthetic opiates. There was also concern about the number of addicted doctors, and about practitioners who were prepared to prescribe inappropriately, and to the feeling that treatment, as opposed to maintenance, was nearly non-existent. The Committee's report was published in April 1961.[18] Its broad conclusions were that there was not too much of a problem, and that no major changes in the existing arrangements were required. Examination of the Committee's extraordinary bland conclusions tell us that there was little desire to read between the lines, or to challenge the information it was given. The Committee appeared to condone the practice of addicted doctors prescribing for their own needs. The soft touch 'script' doctors were felt to be such a difficult subject that they were virtually ignored. Perhaps this report marked the end of innocence.

In spite of the complacent findings of the Brain Committee, the drug scene in Britain was changing fast. The government had reported to the United Nations in 1950, that cannabis (then still called Indian hemp) had become a more important problem than traffic in opium. It was no longer confined to the West Indian population and was becoming increasingly popular in music and dance clubs. It had also become clear by this time that there was a new group of drugs on the menu – amphetamines.

Stimulant drugs, like amphetamines, were mentioned by the first Brain Committee only to be dismissed, in spite of some disturbing evidence. They were being widely used as a treatment for depression because they were regarded as 'safe and non-addictive', and they were sold over the counter without a prescription. Their illicit consumption was well-known to the pharmaceutical fraternity, who lobbied for action, but it took until 1964 for the government to do anything about it. Initial concern focused on the prescription of amphetamines by doctors to patients with mental illness, rather than on the increasing use of un-prescribed 'pep pills' – the most popular being 'purple hearts'. Their use by young people in nightclubs initiated the culture which was eventually to lead to ecstasy and other 'rave' drugs.

The government's response was The Drugs (Prevention of Misuse) Act of 1964. It was a sticking plaster on a gaping wound. It made possession of amphetamines an offence, but not supply, leaving the police with the necessity to obtain proof-of-sale in order to charge a dealer. The bill was ill-considered and ineffective. It was a political knee-jerk reaction to the need to 'do something' and to be seen to be 'doing something'. It acted as a palliative, delaying more effective amphetamines control until 1971.

The Inspectorate of Drugs at the Home Office became increasingly concerned by the scale of heroin abuse. Problems were mostly in London, where over-prescription was beginning to fuel the black market. An improbable figure, Lady Isabella Frankau, was largely responsible. In 1957, as a psychiatrist running a private practice for the treatment of alcoholics, she struck up an arrangement with another colleague with some experience in the field, to treat heroin addicts. But her prescribing became increasingly eccentric.

Lady Frankau was certainly not alone in prescribing for addicts. Some were very responsible, but the evidence at the time was strong that the black market in heroin depended on the sale of over-generous prescriptions, which in large part paid for the addict's habit. This was an embarrassment to the government in view of its international obligations to suppress addiction and everything that fed it.

In spite of the clearest evidence of irresponsible prescribing by a few doctors, until the beginning of the 1970s there was   an extraordinary reluctance on the part of the authorities to do anything about it. The Rolleston Committee had suggested that a tribunal of suitable doctors should be set up to deal with instances when a doctor's prescribing for addicts gave cause for concern. Astonishingly no such tribunal was ever convened. Attitudes were probably influenced by the failure, in 1955, to obtain a conviction against a Dr Rourke on the grounds that the regulations gave 'absolute discretion' to doctors to prescribe as they felt proper for the treatment of their patients. The bizarre reluctance to address this problem is best epitomized by the view of the Chief Legal Adviser at the Home Office that the problem of Lady Frankau would be solved 'by the effluxion of time' – a statement worthy of Sir Humphrey in *Yes Minister*.

In 1964, Lord Brain was persuaded to chair the second Brain Committee. Its terms of reference were restricted to concerns about over-prescription of heroin and cocaine. Although Lord Brain was greatly in favour of tribunals, he was in the end overruled by senior officials who still maintained that if a case were strong enough it should be dealt with by the courts. In the end it was agreed that the General Medical Council's powers should be extended to allow it to review a doctor's fitness to 'possess, supply and prescribe dangerous drugs'. The Committee reported in July 1965, and recommended that there should be compulsory notification of addicts to the Home Office, that there should be special centres set up for the treatment of addicts, and that restrictions should be placed on doctors to prescribe heroin and cocaine for addicts outside these special centres.

The time between the second Brain Committee's report, published in November 1965,[19] and the Dangerous Drugs Act of 1967, which gave substance to the recommendations, saw the emergence of the drug problem as we know it today. The first known heroin addict under the age of 20 was reported in 1960, but by 1967 there were 381 known users in that age group. 1965 to 1967 saw all that change. The number of known addicts increased two-and-a-half times, and heroin from abroad made its appearance on the black market.

The drafting of the Dangerous Drugs Act of 1967 ran into problems. The General Medical Council proved unwilling to take on the role recommended for it in relation to 'inappropriate prescribing', and the British Medical Association balked at the proposed restrictions on prescribing by doctors. In the end the Act provided for a tribunal to consider failure to notify addicts, and heroin prescription by unlicensed doctors, but no such tribunal was ever convened. The Department of Health was responsible for setting up the new special treatment centres, without which reasonable provision for addicts' care could not be made. This was an urgent problem because many general practitioners, seeing that their freedom to prescribe for addicts was about to be curtailed, decided that they could no longer see such patients. It proved to be a saga of muddle, procrastination, unclear objectives, lack of enthusiasm from some quarters, and disagreement about funding.

It also emerged that there was extraordinarily little professional expertise in treating, as opposed to prescribing for, addicts. Every psychiatrist was assumed to know all about the problems. In reality the great majority did not wish to have anything to do with addicts, and knew nothing about the subject. The Chief Medical Officer at the Department of Health, Sir George Godber, by a mixture of astute flattery and deft politics, got an agreement with psychiatrists that the centres would be set up, mostly in London teaching hospitals. There was also widespread uncertainty as to what a treatment centre should consist of. The hapless Minister of Health, Kenneth Robinson, had to stonewall repeatedly with statements about 'urgent consultations' and other parliamentary anodynes. There were references to the number of centres 'already in existence' which backbenchers and the press failed to identify. Meanwhile, those in day-to-day contact with addicts and their problems continued to trumpet the complete failure to provide practical help. The Dangerous Drugs Act reached the statute book in October 1967, and came into force early in 1968.

In January 1967, there were 659 addicts known to the Home Office, of which 86 per cent gave a London address. The Minister of Health told Parliament six months later that they were planning that 'perhaps' one thousand addicts would seek treatment, and that this figure might drop with 'imminent legislation'. The truth was that nobody knew what was needed. Furthermore, the civil servants at the Department of Health did not need to be reminded that their primary duty was to protect their Minister. Fancy footwork was more important than the need to solve problems.

Nevertheless, in April 1968, fifteen treatment centres were opened in London, almost all attached to teaching hospitals, with a few in towns near London. They were in the main, dedicated out-patient departments. Some order was restored as soon as all prescriptions for injectable methyl-amphetamine (Methedrine) were stopped, and the centres ceased, with very rare exceptions, to prescribe cocaine. Within two years, the Chief Inspector at the Home Office reported that cocaine was so unfashionable that 'you couldn't even give it away'.

Prescribing free illegal drugs to addicts was a continuation of the principles sanctioned by the 1926 Rolleston Committee. The intention was to limit the spread of heroin addiction by controlled availability, rather than allowing an uncontrolled black market to develop. It had served both addicts and society well, largely because there were so few of them. It had become known as the 'British system'. In truth it was not a carefully considered policy, but more an administratively simple way of dealing with what was then a small problem. Its lasting value was precisely because it was not a system based on legislation, or even on edicts from the Ministry of Health. The non-system allowed a measure of experimentation and flexibility, and ensured that the management of addicts remained a medical, not a legal, concern. It explains why, even today, there is great freedom to prescribe opiate substitutes in the form and dose thought by the prescriber to be most suitable for an individual, rather than imposing a single rigid treatment programme. Its early success was probably due to the bourgeois middle class nature of the addicts. But as the numbers of addicts rose during the 1960s and 1970s, and their reasons for taking drugs changed, its intended purpose was shown to have failed, and less and less was heard about the merits of the 'British system'.

Into this vacuum of knowledge and experience emerged the Hospital Memorandum on the 'Treatment and Supervision of Heroin Addiction', issued by the Ministry of Health in 1967.[20] It recognized that if addicts were denied heroin they would return to the black market, which would prosper as a consequence. It therefore provided for continued supply of properly controlled amounts of heroin to addicts who either could not or would not give up, and for those in a reduction programme.

The treatment centres did not get off to a promising start. For the first few years of their existence injectable heroin was prescribed more or less on demand, but prescribing policy seems to have been dictated by fashion rather than by evidence. In the early 1970s, this tended to be replaced by injectable methadone, which was considered to be medicine, whereas heroin was objectionable on the Alice in Wonderland grounds that it was hedonistic and abusable. In about 1977, this gave way to oral methadone, because it was believed that injecting was neither morally nor medically good for patients. In any case, injectable methadone had not proved popular with entrenched addicts, who tended to sell their ampoules on the black market in order to buy street heroin. This, of course, kept the illicit market well supplied with methadone ampoules, but heroin was getting more expensive and difficult to find as treatment centres ceased to prescribe it. Consequently, addicts turned to other drugs such as dipipanone (Diconal), barbiturates and methyl-phenidate (Ritalin).

Treatment centres signally failed in preventing both an increase in the number of addicts, and the spread of the black market: so much for their role in containment and social control. Many doctors were getting increasingly frustrated and demoralized at being mere prescription writers for 'patients' who did not consider themselves to be ill or in need of treatment. After a particularly inconclusive meeting of treatment centre consultants in 1976, the Chief Inspector at the Home Office, 'Bing' Spear, a legendary figure who wrote a uniquely authoritative account of the twists and turns of drug politics, noted that 'it was remarkable for the fact that there was, after eight years, no clear idea what they were trying to achieve, or how they should go about it.'[21]

In July 1966, a proposal of the second Brain Committee to set up a standing advisory committee on addiction was duly implemented as the Advisory Committee on Drug Dependency. It took time to get into its stride, but it reached far-sighted conclusions based on common sense. One of its earliest actions was to set up a subcommittee under the chairmanship of Baroness (Barbara) Wooton to prepare a report on the increasing use of cannabis, which was causing concern. It issued a report, full also of common sense.[22] It concluded that there was no evidence for many of the then current beliefs, though it saw no alternative to continued restrictions on its availability.

But, of course, events were moving very much faster than policy. The numbers of heroin addicts were rising fast, and pockets of addiction were evident outside London. The black market was once again thriving on imported heroin, and amphetamines became the new craze. The high priest of the moment was Dr John Peto. He prescribed heroin in over-generous quantities, and methyl-amphetamine, initially in the form of pills, but then as an intravenous injection, which he believed would stop cocaine use. Having been hounded out of Wimpole Street, he practiced from an ever-changing succession of sleazy hotels, and finally from the refreshment room at Baker Street station, before he was, eventually, struck off the register.

The 1967 Dangerous Drugs Act was soon recognized to be flawed. Narcotic drugs were being used in ever-larger quantities, and their range was extending. Legal remedies were inadequate; events were overtaking legislation. In 1971, the Misuse of Drugs Act was passed, which remains in force today. It introduced the ABC classification of drugs, with different penalties for dealing and possession in each class, based on the harms thought to flow from their use. There have been some subsequent changes in the classification, and some of them remain controversial. The Act also recommended replacing the Advisory Council on Drug Dependency with a new body, the Advisory Council on the Misuse of Drugs. The Misuse of Drugs regulations in 1985 ordered the way prescriptions were to be written, and introduced the 'Controlled Drugs Register', and the concept of 'prescription only drugs'.

The years between the late 1960s and 1984 saw mounting evidence of serious drug problems met by a stupefying complacency and disinclination to take any effective action. There was a brief fashion for the misuse of metha-qualone or Mandrax, and a much bigger and more dangerous problem with barbiturates, which killed more users than heroin. It took a full five years to bring barbiturates under the control of the Misuse of Drugs Act, following a recommendation of the Advisory Council. It took fourteen years, until 1984, before Diconal was controlled.

In 1973, cocaine made its appearance on the black market. Heroin was becoming more popular and by 1978 it had migrated north to Edinburgh. There was trouble ahead for anyone who wished to see it, but the authorities did not want to look. The Chief Inspector wrote that, 'the cloud of complacency which has once more settled on the Home Office, the Department of Health, the ACMD and the medical profession was impenetrable". By the early 1980s, numbers were again rising fast, particularly in Scotland and Merseyside, and armed thefts from wholesalers and pharmacies, clearly the work of professional criminals, were reported. Once again something had to be done.

In 1984, the government set up an inter-departmental group on the misuse of drugs, under the chairmanship of David Mellor, then a junior minister at the Home Office. Its recommendations laid the foundations for all subsequent drug policy, and identified a much greater role for central government in seeking to stop drugs from reaching Britain: further tightening controls on drugs produced or prescribed in the country; increasing the effectiveness of policing; strengthening deterrence to trafficking and dealing, and improving all aspects of treatment.[24]

In 1982 meanwhile, the Advisory Council published its long-awaited report entitled 'Treatment and Rehabilitation'.[25] Seven years in the making, it was worth the wait. Taking the approach to the management of addiction in a new direction, it recognized the effects of past under-funding, and noted that many addicts were seeking treatment from general practitioners, because of 'profound differences in professional opinions on the prescribing of opiates.' It concluded that treatment centres should give way to Community Drug Teams, which should involve the traditional care providers – GPs, social services, voluntary and charitable non-statutory services, and hospital-based specialists. As the new Community Drug Teams struggled uncertainly to their feet, the NHS, following the Griffiths Management Enquiry, was changing. The hitherto unchallenged primacy of doctors in policy-making was leaking away, and new groups of non-medical professionals were being recruited. What Theodore

Dalrymple has disparaged as the new 'addiction bureaucracy' was being born.[26]

In October 1984, 'Guidelines for good practice in the treatment of drug misuse' were issued and sent to all doctors.[27] Subsequent versions were published – 1991,[28] 1999[29] – and in 2007.[30] The document expressed the hope that significant numbers of GPs would become involved, but almost none were prepared to take up the challenge. But the Guidelines were exactly that – guidelines – and the authorities recognized that nonconformity and irresponsibility were not the same thing.

The year 1985 saw the outbreak of HIV among injecting addicts in eastern Scotland. Its catastrophic potential was immediately recognized. The ACMD courageously and rightly reported that, 'HIV is a greater threat to public and individual health than drug misuse.'[31] Needle exchanges were piloted and rolled-out with commendable speed, following a very hard-hitting publicity campaign. This response represents about the only triumph in British drug policy – other countries fared much worse.

The HIV outbreak undoubtedly changed the thinking about the treatment of drug abuse. Drug taking was no longer just a minority deviant behaviour, but a major personal and public health concern. It was recognized that prescribing injectables might be legitimate as a necessary temporary measure. And for the first time, stress was laid on the benefits of methadone maintenance for those not yet willing or able to consider abstinence. This, in turn, served to make it obvious that large areas of the country were devoid of any acceptable treatment facilities at all. The government responded with the Central Funding Initiative.

If the HIV outbreak had been well handled, the same cannot be said in the case of Hepatitis C. It, too, is a highly contagious disease spread by needle sharing, or in the earliest cases, by transfusions of blood containing the virus. The government declined to fund an investigation by the ACMD, and it was only action by pressure groups that eventually goaded the government into reacting. There are thought to be three to four hundred thousand infected individuals in the country, and treatment is very expensive, at about £15,000 per patient. The only alternative to treatment is a liver transplant, and it is now government policy to treat all those infected.

In 1994, yet another Task Force was set up to examine all aspects of services for drug misusers and drug policy. This time the chairman was the remarkable John Polkinghorne, then President of Queen's College Cambridge, a theoretical physicist, Fellow of the Royal Society and a Church of England priest. It was a response to the general sense of concern that not enough was being done, and an unease in certain quarters that methadone, not abstinence, was the main thrust of treatment. The report was full of common sense, and broadly confirmed the general direction of policy.[32] It also commissioned important research, and paved the way for increasing involvement of the criminal justice system in initiating treatment.

By the year 2000, treatment services had once again become fragmented and demoralized under endless financial pressures, and the move to devolve services – local autonomy was the byword. In 2001, the National Treatment Agency for Substance Abuse was set up as a Special Health Authority, 'to improve the availability, capacity and effectiveness of treatment for drug misuse in England.'

The first National Drug Strategy was published in 1995.[33] It replaced Community Drug Teams with Drug Action Teams, which were to commission services rather than to provide them themselves. This was followed, in 1998, by the first ten-year strategy entitled, 'Tackling Drugs Together for a Better Britain'.[34] As discussed in Chapter 3, both it and its successor, 'Drugs: Protecting Families and Communities', published in 2008,[35] are worthy, uncontroversial wish-lists, but neither introduced any new thinking of the kind which might break the mould. We are still waiting for that. On the positive side, there has been a very useful emphasis on reducing the harms that flow from drugs and drug taking, both to individuals and to society. Less welcome has been the extent to which recent governments have abandoned evidence in favour of politics, most obviously in the reclassification of cannabis against the advice of its own Advisory Council on the Misuse of Drugs.[36]

Of concern, too, is the generally low standard of treatment for addicts, though there are very welcome exceptions. There are some striking figures from both sides of the Atlantic showing what good value for money treatment is. In Britain, every pound spent on treatment for opiate abuse repays between £9.50 and £18, depending upon how the effects of crime are costed.[37] In America, a study by the Rand Corporation found that every dollar spent on the treatment of cocaine users yielded $7.48.[38] The tragedy is that, at least in Britain, much of the treatment offered is of such poor quality, with so little engagement of the addict, as to make it impossible to reap such benefits.

It is depressing that exceptionally demanding requirements for supervised daily consumption are frequently regarded as more important than being in a job, which is one of the most important elements of beginning to sustain an abstinent life. Indeed, it is common to require someone in work who enters treatment to give up his job. These returns on the money invested in treatment are many times the returns from any of the other anti-drug activities on which the government spends money. There is a strong case for scaling back some of these marginally effective but expensive measures, and spending the money saved bringing the standards of treatment up to the best.

During a discussion I had recently with an addict in treatment, he made the eminently sensible statement that it ought to be easier to get a doctor to write a prescription for methadone than for an addict to buy heroin from the black market. Sadly, this has never been the case and is only exceptionally the case now. Just how difficult this can be is illustrated by the shocking story of Peter Wayne, recounted in *The Week* magazine.[39] Wayne left prison at the end of his sentence determined to kick his twenty-year heroin habit, and get a job. He had been given the name of a drug agency, and immediately went there to get help – and a dose of methadone. It became a bureaucratic nightmare because he did not have a general practitioner, having been in prison for twenty years, who may or may not have been persuaded to prescribe. The agency required two weeks of form filling, urine testing, and referral elsewhere. It would be another six weeks before anyone might give him a prescription. Inevitably he resumed using street heroin, was re-arrested, and thankful to return to his methadone prescription in prison.

The United Nations, and its predecessor the League of Nations, have played a leading part in the worldwide fight against all aspects of the international drug trade. Ever since the 1912 Hague International Opium Convention, there have been conventions and protocols on different aspects of the global problem, most notably the 1961 Single Convention on Narcotic Drugs, and the 1971 Convention on Psychotropic Substances. These treaties had to reconcile very differing views, but were always prohibitionist in tone, and heavily influenced by America.

This chapter has considered in some detail the evolution of drug policy in America and in Britain. In many ways, policies in the two countries are very different. Those in America seem to have been driven by an ideology without much regard for the realities. In Britain, on the other hand, policies have evolved as a series of reactions to events, often inadequate and too late. What unites them is that both are anchored in the premise that narcotic drugs are illegal because the law prohibits them. It is precisely because of this arbitrary prohibition that neither has had any real success in containing the problem. There are no examples from the past of successful permanent suppression by government *fiat* of a habit enjoyed by millions of citizens. And there is no likelihood that there ever will be.

3   Own Goals and Other Absurdities – why we do not get better drug policies

Sometimes legislation does not achieve the purposes intended. Very occasionally, a bill debated in Parliament and passed into law, actually has the effect of promoting those ends which it was intended to prevent. This perversity is seen in the implementation of drug policy probably more than in any other field. Of course, not every action in the fight against drugs is governed by legislation, but it is quite remarkable how often a well-meant and apparently sensible decision backfires, and leads to highly undesirable consequences. Stated in other words, it scores an own goal. Why this particular field of endeavour should be so subject to such outcomes is something worth thinking about. It is not because such a perverse outcome could not have been predicted. Indeed, quite the contrary – it was often predictable. Why, therefore, was it not considered when action was proposed? We are driven to the depressing conclusion that no one really thinks about it, or that those taking the decisions do not know enough about the subject to see the dangers. There are plenty of examples.

In the previous chapter we saw that the rise of prohibition in America and the two Supreme Court judgements of 1919 and 1922 made it impossible for doctors to attempt to wean addicts off opiates with diminishing doses. And the 1922 Jones-Miller Act and the 1924 Porter Act forbade the importation or manufacture of heroin. The opiate addicts of America, of which there were many thousands, were left with no legal source of drugs. Naturally and predictably, many of them became small-time dealers of illegally acquired opiates, which the efficient criminal world soon provided. These new and reluctant dealers went about recruiting new users and selling to them, so increasing the number of addicts.

The most extraordinary and important own goal ever scored in the field of drug control was the direct consequence of US government action taken shortly after President Nixon declared his 'War on Drugs'. There was an urgency and ruthlessness about his actions at this time. He clearly believed that drugs were a direct threat to the cohesion of American society, but he was also keen to direct attention away from the war in Vietnam, which at that time was not going well. He took his inspiration from Vietnam, where thousands of tonnes of defoliants had been dropped on the forests in an attempt to deny the Vietcong cover to conceal their movements. He sought permission to use the same aerial spraying to destroy the extensive poppy and marijuana crops in Mexico, south of the US border. Mexico did not accede to this request. Rebuffed, Nixon decided to close the 2,300 miles of the US-Mexican border. Hundreds of thousands of people and vehicles were searched, and millions of Americans, whose lives were in no way incommoded, applauded this 'tough' action. Most small growers of marijuana in Mexico went out of business because they were no longer able to get their products safely across the border to the large numbers of migrant workers for whom its use was a normal and harmless part of life.

Nobody seems to learn anything from the past. Over time, the inevitable happened. More and more people, both Mexicans and Americans, started to grow marijuana in well-concealed plots in the mountains and canyons of California and elsewhere. Thirty-five years later, marijuana had become the largest cash crop in America by value, exceeding that of maize. Nixon's action had ultimately resulted in the importation of a whole criminal industry, thus making it greatly more difficult to control. It can be argued whether or not this was a predictable consequence, but it should at least have been considered as a possibility. We do not know if it was.

This was not just an American phenomenon. In the early 1980s there was much concern in the big cities of Scotland at the number of addicts who were choosing to inject their drugs into a vein. A consensus emerged among retail chemists that they would no longer sell the small 2ml. syringes that the addicts used to take their drugs. In this way it would become impossible to continue this undesirable and dangerous habit, or so they thought. The result was totally different, and catastrophic. Denied access to the small syringes which each addict had previously for his or her own use, they bought 20ml. syringes, which were still sold by the chemists. Five or so users would meet, cook up their heroin solution and pass the syringe round. Each of them would draw a little blood back into the syringe to ensure that they were in a vein, then inject their dose. All but the first would, therefore, be injecting a little blood as well as the heroin, and the last in the line would have put the blood of four other addicts into his or her system.

There are two serious diseases prevalent among intravenous drug users. One is Hepatitis C, the most virulent type of Hepatitis, which has lasting consequences, and can lead ultimately to death, though rarely. The other is AIDS, and this needle-sharing behaviour in Scotland led to the outbreak of a small epidemic of this terrible disease.

Another own goal: it might, perhaps, be considered a good idea to test the urine of those in prison to determine the extent of drug taking, and to be able to offer users some help to become abstinent. At one time, random testing was more or less routine, but it had quite unexpected and undesirable consequences. Testing is done by dipping the end of a credit card sized test kit into a specimen of urine. After a minute or two it will register the presence or absence of any of the ten most commonly used illegal drugs. The problem is that drugs remain in the system, and hence in the urine, for differing lengths of time. Heroin, for example, will show positive for about five days after its last use. But even one smoke of cannabis will be detectable for up to 21 days, and longer if it is used regularly. In circumstances where the presence of a drug might result in sanctions, or the withdrawal of privileges, such as in prison, there is a very clear advantage in using heroin rather than cannabis. On the basis of random testing, you are much less likely to be caught after using heroin, or any other opiate, than you are if you smoke the occasional joint. But, of course, opiates have a much greater potential for harm than cannabis. Indeed, some prison officers feel that cannabis-smoking makes inmates less aggressive and more compliant, and hence easier to control. Thus, a seemingly sensible idea turns out to be totally counter-productive. Routine urine testing has now been dropped in British prisons.

Very similar thinking resulted in these tests being used in a few schools. The children very quickly learned that they should avoid cannabis, and, although heroin use in schools is certainly not common, there is a range of other illegal drugs, all of which are considerably more problematic and damaging than the odd smoke of cannabis. These facts have been known for quite a long time, and any joined-up thinking would have made these undesirable effects predictable. Once again there was no well-informed consideration before action was taken.

Drug education in schools has turned out to be an unexpectedly contentious issue. In principle, it is clearly a 'good thing' to inform children about the evils of drugs, and school is the obvious place to do it, but it has not proved at all easy to do this effectively. Early efforts were pathetically counter-productive. In a misplaced attempt to make drugs unattractive, dire but untrue consequences of taking drugs were described. When, in due course, some rebellious children did actually take the drug and found that the reputed effects did not follow, the teachers who had issued the warnings were regarded as not knowing what they were talking about, and they became figures of fun who could not be trusted, whatever they were talking about.

For some time anti-drug propaganda, for such is what it was, never mentioned the fact that drugs could be enjoyable. Considering that this is the main reason for taking a drug, this omission was ridiculous and devalued the warnings which followed, however reasonable or sensible they were. Such teachers were obviously spoilsports. Much more thought has been given to the subject recently, but an evaluation of the latest thinking, enshrined in the elaborate and long-awaited 'Blueprint' project,[40] was unable to demonstrate that it had any measurable effect. This was a great disappointment, and consequently the whole subject has lost momentum, placing more importance on how parents talk to their children about drug use. It would be a great mistake to believe that this is an easy subject.

One of the stated objectives of prohibiting illegal drugs is to drive up the price, and so make it impossible for all but the most wealthy to support a habit. But expensive drugs, whatever the cause of the price rise, always lead to more dangerous habits. Drugs can become more expensive for many reasons – effective police action, though this is always temporary; drought in producer countries; or a shortage locally, for example in a prison. Faced with higher prices, any addict is going to ensure that he or she gets the biggest buzz for the money spent. If we take heroin as an example, only 14 per cent of the substance smoked in a cigarette produces an effect in the body, while the rest is 'wasted'. On the other hand, inhaling the fumes from heroin melted on aluminium foil ('chasing the dragon') yields about 25 per cent. But intravenous injection is more than two and a half times as effective than this.[41] It should come as no surprise that high prices lead to more injecting, which is much more dangerous than inhaling. From time to time even the most experienced addicts make mistakes with their doses, and once it has been injected it cannot be recovered. Virtually all deaths due to overdoses of heroin follow injection, and the process of injecting brings other dangers. Thrombosis of the leg veins is common, and blood-borne infections which can destroy the heart valves, and tuberculosis, are regularly seen in injecting addicts because they are giving themselves unsterile dose

There have been recent reports[42] of a particularly disturbing and horrific consequence of high heroin prices. The authorities in Russia have had some success in halting the flow of Afghan heroin into Russia through Tajikistan, Kyrgyzstan and Kazakhstan, which has resulted in higher prices. Those who are unable to afford heroin have been using a drug which is easily made at home from codeine – readily available over the counter – iodine, lighter fluid, and industrial cleaning oil. A 'hit' is many times cheaper than heroin. It is known as 'krokodil', a reference to the fact that it eats away flesh. It causes extensive tissue death whenever it is injected outside a vein, which often happens. The skin turns green and rots away, revealing infected underlying tissues, and even bare bone. There are terrible video-clips of the damage it does to be seen by Googling 'krokodil'. There can be no more convincing or dramatic evidence of the total failure of high prices as a mechanism to stop addicts using drugs, and harming themselves. They would be many times better off using heroin. High prices always lead to more risky and damaging behaviour by those who are still in thrall to drugs. Expensive drugs may choke off demand from the older and more mature users, who are, in any case, getting nearer to the end of their drug careers.

Of course, things are not always predictable. In 2001, there was a severe heroin drought in Australia, thought to have been due to a particularly effective campaign by police and customs officers, and a coincidental change in the production and distribution of heroin in South East Asia. It certainly put prices up, but paradoxically, opiate overdoses and deaths fell. This is probably because Australian addicts responded to higher prices differently from their British counterparts. They took enthusiastically to using methyl-amphetamine ('crystal meth' or 'ice', a drug which to date is little used in Britain), injecting it, together with cocaine, a behaviour causing all the complications mentioned above, and a high incidence of psychiatric problems. They also took to making large amounts of 'homebake' from any codeine-containing painkiller, which could be bought easily over the counter. It proved to be just as addictive as heroin, to which it is chemically closely related.

Another consequence of high prices is that users who are priced out of the market resort to cheaper but sometimes more dangerous alternative drugs. Worse still, some start to drink alcohol heavily, while also taking a cocktail of whatever other drugs they can get hold of. This is a particularly dangerous, and even a lethal, thing to do. It is ironic that on the rare occasions when prohibition is successful, the damage to users' health and the number of drug-related deaths increase.

There is another situation Nixon never envisaged. High drug prices can, paradoxically, lead to an increase in the local drug using population. When heroin prices rise there still will be a price that some users will struggle to afford. They are faced with three choices – they could give up drugs altogether; temporarily or permanently seek other drugs, perhaps street methadone; or decide to subsidize their now-expensive habit by becoming a dealer.

Dealers can certainly make good money if they are prepared to take the risk, and some will. But that means that they will have to find customers. Most users will already have a dealer with whom they do business, and sometimes more than one. To lure users away from their dealer can be risky, for rough justice and violence are never far below the surface. A safer option is to work hard with the young and impressionable in the hope and expectation that some of them can be groomed until they acquire a habit. These will be new users recruited because the new dealer has to find new clients. Some of them would never have become users were it not for the pressure and persistence of the new dealer to sustain his or her habit, and in this way the number of users in the area will increase. In all likelihood a few of the new recruits will also become dealers for the same reason, and so the cycle continues.

Governments seem to have a problem with the existence of opium dens. Not surprising perhaps, they are not a part of most people's culture. But they have long been a part of life in Chinese communities, and, furthermore, they have kept themselves to themselves, and for the most part have not attracted non-Chinese custom. The first instinct of all governments is to close them down and so rid their cities of this evil and decadent stain. But, of course, such action does not stop the displaced clientele smoking opium –

it merely drives it underground and makes it more difficult to control.

Such a course of action indicates a total lack of understanding of the nature of addiction – a mistake made time and time again by the authorities all over the world whenever they confront goings on of which they do not approve. It is a knee-jerk reaction, and the result is always the same, whether in San Francisco in the 1870s, Manila in the 1890s, or Bangkok and elsewhere in the 1970s. The devotees of opium smoking simply take to using heroin when denied opium, and so swell the numbers of customers queuing up to buy it from the gangs of criminals who make it their business to produce and distribute heroin and prosper obscenely by doing so. Furthermore, heroin smoke lacks any distinctive smell, unlike opium smoke, making detection much more difficult. Another own goal which could have been avoided by some foresight before action was taken.

Nobody could expect illegal drugs to get a good press, and they have no defenders. The world would be a much better place without them, and we should never forget that. But, like it or not, they are a reality and they have assumed an importance in many people's lives. Many of the articles on the subject are very partisan, displaying no comprehension of the nature of addiction, and the way addicts behave. But there are others that, by and large, present the facts in good faith without any systematic attempt to distort them. Such has not always been the case. There has, in the past, been a very conscious attempt to demonize drugs, and so the thinking went, to make them less attractive to potential users. It was an interesting idea.

Demonization means that the subject is no longer to be regarded as 'normal', and so is deprived of the right to dispassionate consideration. This 'exile of convenience' then defers the necessity or obligation to face up to the issues involved. Demonization is achieved by use of language and images which associate their subject with loathsomeness, hatred and fear. It is implied that dark and evil forces are at work, and that those who choose to venture into that world are depraved, and that their mortal souls are in danger. This process is rather akin to what is now called 'securitization'. As soon as something is said to be a threat to security it enters a world where the rules are quite different. It becomes an emergency which must be dealt with quickly, and often outside normal democratic rules and regulations.

The Victorian Temperance Movement understood this process well, and played upon people's fears of the extremities of degradation to which 'demon drink' could reduce you, and your innocent wife and children. It also implied that the evil comes from outside normal society – that it was not home-grown, but the product of something that we do not understand. This foreignness in Britain focused on the 'yellow peril' and the opium dens of the Chinese, while in America it was the Mexicans who were responsible for all the evils of marijuana; to this day it is known by its Spanish or Mexican name, and not as cannabis.

Harry Anslinger, the first head of the US Federal Bureau of Narcotics, was an effective practitioner of demonization, but he had motives other than trying to put people off drugs. He was intensely ambitious and saw exaggeration, combined with public credulity, as a way of enhancing his personal reputation as the protector of the public from this evil, and of getting more federal funds for his department. He was very successful. He wrote, for example, that 'some people will fly into a delirious rage and may commit violent crimes' under the influence of marijuana. He told another story of a marijuana 'addict' who 'turned his house into a human slaughterhouse' by killing his parents, brother and sister with an axe. He speculated 'how many murders, suicides, robberies, criminal assaults, hold-ups, burglaries and deeds of maniacal insanity it causes every year, especially among the young . . .'

Anslinger also wrote a book entitled *Marijuana: Assassin of Youth* which made wildly exaggerated assertions about the extremities of criminal and sexual behaviour to which marijuana could drive you. To anyone who knows anything about the effects of cannabis today these statements are laughable. But Harry Anslinger was not the only person riding this bandwagon.

In 1938, a Federal Bureau of Narcotics agent warned a journalist that 'an overdose of marijuana generates savage and sadistic traits likely to reach a climax in axe and ice-pick murders.' When a judge passed sentence on a man for transgression of the Marijuana Tax Bill, he committed him to jail for four years and fined him $1,000, and he said, 'I consider marijuana the worst of all narcotics – far worse than the use of morphine and cocaine. Marijuana destroys life itself.'

This kind of departure from reality had started much earlier. Hamilton Wright, an ambitious Washington doctor, who was a delegate at the 1909 Shanghai Opium Commission, wrote to the Archbishop of Canterbury stating that morphine addiction was a greater problem in some American states than opium-smoking in China. In his report to Congress on the deliberations of the Commission, he raised lurid and baseless concerns about cocaine debauchery by blacks in the Southern states. Dr Salam El Guindy, the Egyptian delegate to the League of Nations Second Opium Conference in 1925, sought to add cannabis to the list of prohibited narcotics on the grounds that it was 'at least as harmful as opium, if not more so', and he reported that cannabis was responsible for 'between 30 per cent and 60 per cent of the total number of cases of insanity in Egypt.' The true figure, subsequently discovered, was 3 per cent of admissions to mental hospitals, several times less than those attributed to alcohol.

This theatre of the absurd continues today. In 1989, President Bush Senior's 'Drug Tsar' claimed that his proposals would reduce drug use in America by 50 per cent by 1999.

We have seen that one of the objectives of the British 1998 Drug

Policy was to reduce Afghan opium production by 70 per cent by 2007, and that it would be eliminated entirely by 2012.[43] These targets have been quietly dropped. Extraordinary proposals were made by Tony Blair's special advisor considering the problems of heroin. There was to be widespread prescription of free heroin to ensure that addicts did not have to commit crimes to finance their habits, while at the same time making it illegal to use, as well as to possess, heroin. Chaotic users were to be 'captured and gripped' in coerced treatment. Non-compliance with treatment would usually attract a prison sentence. Presumably the author of this document, Lord Birt, had been told that there were more than 300,000 heroin addicts and 70,000 places in prison. Furthermore, the proposals seem to have overlooked the fact that prisons are the universities of drug taking. Unsurprisingly, publication of these proposals was suppressed for a time.

To cap all this, in 1998 the United Nations committed 150 member nations, including Britain, to the most strenuous efforts to eradicate all coca, opium and cannabis from the planet by 2008. That the UN could think that the planet will ever be free of these products shows a naivety and ignorance which is seriously alarming. It also tells us that in this particular talking shop there is no serious intent to tackle the worldwide problem of drug use.

These stories are not isolated. They are, collectively, a litany of absurdity extending back over many years. Wishful thinking, fantasy and ignorance of the facts will never contribute to policy which has the slightest chance of success. One must ask why supposedly sensible individuals and public bodies have continued to have such scant regard for truth and reality. We have seen that, in the case of some individuals, the motive is self-serving or personal aggrandizement. On other occasions one can suppose that pronouncements are made for reasons of political expediency, in the belief that memories are short and people will forget what was said. But sometimes one is left floundering even to suggest why a particular statement was made.

A case in point is the United Nations 'drug-free planet'. Nobody with even the haziest knowledge of the situation could possibly believe that the world would have made notable progress towards a drug-free world by 2008. If anyone did believe this to be possible they had no business to take part in such a debate. It can only be that a headline-grabbing statement was thought to be necessary, and that the need for a ringing and optimistic call-to-arms was more important than logic or reason. If so, it is depressing for, once again, the sound bite has trumped reality.

Does it really matter if a few people make absurd public statements? It does matter, because it becomes much more difficult to have a well-informed, rational and dispassionate discussion. It is at present difficult to debate many aspects of national drug policy because the language tends to become extreme, and the argument irrational, or even hysterical. We do not find this difficulty with, for example, discussions about educational policy or the future of health care in Britain. We must dissipate the heat and let the light of reason into the debate.

The rest of this chapter tries to identify reasons why we do not have better and more robust anti-drug policies. It could be that we have found a clue. If the United Nations can disregard the realities of the drug situation in the world, perhaps everyone else is doing the same thing too. Maybe because the whole subject is so difficult, nobody wants to work with facts because they are so discouraging. Policy in this field at present is immature – it needs to grow up and face the unvarnished truth. It needs to get real. Then, perhaps, we might be forced to conclude that we have to do something different, for what has gone before patently has not had much positive effect.

There is one overriding reason why prohibition as a general principal of drug control has failed, and always will fail. There is simply too much money in the illegal drug business, and there are masses of people who cannot resist trying to get their hands on some of it. Prohibition is a self-fulfilling prophesy: illegality always puts the price of anything up, and the more successful prohibition is, the scarcer the commodity becomes and the higher will be the price. Hence the more money that can be made supplying it. The arrest of small-time drug dealers does little to limit supplies, because there is a small queue of hopefuls waiting to take over. There is obviously a trade-off between the danger of involvement and the money to be made, but, judging by many people's behaviour, the balance is still firmly tipped in favour of risks being worth taking.

Cocaine and heroin are both derived from plants that grow easily in suitable conditions, which are widespread throughout the world. They are not demanding, and they both can produce more than one crop every year. The major producers of coca leaf and raw opium are poor countries and they have become heavily dependent on these two valuable crops to support a lifestyle that even so is only just above subsistence. Because of the illegality of both drugs, which is conferred by prohibition, the price of both is enormously high. This is 'justified' because of the risks of imprisonment and violence inherent in producing and trafficking these drugs. Prices paid at the 'farm gate' in 2006 for cocaine and heroin were £325 and £450 per kilogram respectively. The price paid by a user on the streets of Britain was £51,650 and £75,750 per kilo – a mark-up of 15,700 per cent and 16,700 per cent respectively.[44] By far the biggest share of this huge profit is made by those who traffic the drugs across international borders. By way of contrast, the mark-up on coffee, a comparable commodity grown in some of the same countries, is nearer three times, or 300 per cent. These figures make it easy to understand why drug smuggling is the easiest way in the world to make enormous sums of money.

There are many examples of the extraordinary fortunes accumulated by drug barons. Pablo Escobar, the capo of the notorious Medellin cartel in Bolivia, owned 200 apartments in Florida, an airline and a hotel in Venezuela, an airline in Bogotá, and a number of hotels in Medellin. In addition, his estate outside Medellin had its own zoo, and had 843 on the payroll. In Mexico, the FBI sequestered $18 million in assets and nine luxury cars, including a Bentley, two Maseratis and a three-wheel motorbike with ostrich-skin seats, from one of the bosses of the Gulf cartel.

Although the lure of riches is the paramount reason why any policy based on prohibition will fail, there are other important issues that also must be considered. Any policy must accept that addiction to narcotics exists in all societies, and always will exist. Unless this awkward fact is acknowledged, and until provision is made for the needs of addicts, they will continue turning to illegal and criminally provided supplies. To believe that denying them access to drugs will force all users to become abstinent is absurd. As a prohibitionist drug policy it is self-defeating.

It is also necessary to know quite a lot more about addiction and the ways in which addicts function. Addicts are under a compulsion other people almost never feel. Their whole being becomes focused two or three times a day on another fix, which must be obtained, whatever the cost. If necessary, money must come from theft or mugging, or by prostituting themselves. Any consideration of family or friendship will be abandoned until the overwhelming need has been assuaged. American policy in the past essentially has denied the existence of the problem by making addicts into non-people, and sweeping the problem under the carpet. To the evident surprise of policy makers, users cannot be forced to abstain by any means yet devised. Addicts do give up drugs and become normal, working citizens, indistinguishable from their more sober colleagues. But they will not do this until they have decided that they have had enough of their former lives and habits.

It comes just as much a surprise to many people that most addicts do kick their habits, and that many others go onto drug substitutes that allow them to function entirely normally. It is even more of a revelation that many addicts, even those not in some form of treatment, can, and often do, work or study part time or full time. There are many myths surrounding the use of drugs which only much greater knowledge among the general public can expunge. Many young addicts go through a phase of being chaotic and unreliable, and often a danger to themselves, but most settle down, particularly if they are wise enough to seek some help. Addicts are normal people who have been unfortunate enough to get hooked by, and remain in thrall to, a drug to which they, contrary to popular belief, often struggle long and hard to come off. The great majority of drug addicts are not recognizable as such. The tragedy is that when they finally become abstinent they find that drugs have stolen their youth, and all the experience and emotional development that goes with it, and it is very difficult to make up for that.

There are not many commendable aspects of drug policy, but it is true to say that British policy, at least until recently, fully recognized the nature of addiction and made humane and civilized provision for the needs of addicts even if, at times, it was dictated by fashion rather than rationality. Doctors treating addicts were required to notify the Home Office, after which they could continue to prescribe without interference. This policy remained until 1998 when the Home Office Register was discontinued, but with certain modifications it is still applied today. This system worked well for many years. In the last year or so a contrary wind has begun to blow, and treatment is becoming less good and less effective because the nature of addiction is no longer its guiding principle. Political considerations have become paramount in guiding policy.

There is another feature of anti-drug legislation and policy making which raises fundamental concerns about its true purpose. One would have hoped that it would focus on the most practical and effective ways of countering all aspects of the extremely complex problems which drugs present to society. Those responsible for policy should be advised by experts who share the same objectives, and not by those who have their own personal or political agenda. A glance at the development of drug policy, related in Chapter 2, will show that this desirable objectivity is not always what has informed policy making. In America, between the

1920s and 1966, when the Rockefeller Drug Laws were enacted in New York State, it is clear that policy was designed to appeal to the moral majority who were being fed terrible and largely untrue stories about the desperate evils of drugs. Ordinary citizens of these times had little personal knowledge of drugs and drug taking, and believed the propaganda. It is likely that even some of the legislators believed what they were told, and for the same reasons. Such grandstanding policy, while being applauded by the ignorant, will lead to unworkable and ineffective policy because it has no regard for, and is in no way informed by, the realities of addiction and drug use.

A similar taint has been apparent in British drug policy for some years now. Hitherto, there had been an admirable principle that was restated whenever policy was discussed. It was described as 'evidence-based', and it usually it did take account of evidence. But this has changed, and ministers making pronouncements no longer use the phrase. This is significant because it is true. Perhaps the moment of truth came when the first National Drug Strategy was about to be presented to Parliament in 1998. It had four elements: to help young people resist drugs so that they might fulfil their potential; to protect communities from drug-related anti-social and criminal behaviour; to enable those with drug problems to get treated and live healthy and crime-free lives; and lastly, action to 'stifle the availability of illegal drugs on our streets'. Evidence was needed to tell us which strands of policy were effective, and which were a waste of money and effort, because the policy 'was to be informed and driven by evidence'. Civil servants involved must have acknowledged that the only objective that could be measured was the number of users who had entered treatment. The other elements did not lend themselves to any meaningful measurement or towards other evidence gathering. These, and subsequent reworkings, are admirable aspirations, but they will never submit to analysis by hard evidence. In particular, we have no idea, even today, how to tell which actions are effective in preventing drugs reaching our streets.

Since 1998, a number of decisions, starting with the reclassification of cannabis from Class C to Class B, have been taken for political reasons, and against the scientific evidence provided by the Advisory Council on the Misuse of Drugs.[45,46] This is a learned and apolitical group whose single purpose is to offer scientific and factual advice to the government. The phrase we now hear is the necessity to 'send a message'. Young people, who are supposed to receive the message, pay no attention to drug classification, or to the implied threat of penal consequences. This is for the very logical reason that they cannot see that smoking a joint is a criminal act. It offends no natural principle of justice. It harms nobody, except in certain very rare instances, the person smoking. The only sense in which it is a criminal offence is because the law says it is.

A recent YouGov survey, commissioned by the Royal Society of Arts Commission on Illegal Drugs, Communities and Public Policy, demonstrated that very few users of drugs pay any attention to the classification of a drug, and so 'receive no messages'.[47] Doubtless this 'tough', but wrong-headed decision, to prefer political gestures to listening to evidence, makes some members of the government more comfortable because they feel that they 'have done their duty'. But it comes at a high price – the abandonment of scientific evidence. To crown this disreputable episode, the government dismissed the then recently appointed chairman of the Advisory Council – Professor David Nutt – because he dared to stick to his guns and criticize the government. A number of Council members resigned as a consequence. And it has provoked a debate about the importance of independent advice in many areas of policy making. Once objectivity and unimpeachable evidence are ignored, policy becomes rudderless.

The real problem, though, at the present time is that evidence, increasingly, is inconvenient, because it often conflicts with government policy. It is therefore better not to have any. The government has made its mind up that it will adhere strictly to the prohibitionist policies of the past. For the moment its mind is closed. No clearer evidence of this could be offered than an unguarded statement by the then drugs minister in a public meeting. When asked if the government would be providing funds to a particular research project, he replied, 'No – why would we when we would take no notice of the findings?'

The almost automatic reply by the government to any suggestion that decriminalization or legalization might be worth discussing, is that it is out of the question because, 'our young people must be protected from the evils of drugs' – as if current policy was doing this effectively. There is such stubborn and illogical adherence to this point of view, which can only be compared to the similarly illogical and self-defeating reluctance of an addict to take the necessary steps to move towards abstinence. There are, though, a few very welcome signs that the edifice of prohibition is not as sound as it was. Recently, Bob Ainsworth, former Home Office minister responsible for drugs policy, came out in favour of a radical shift in our approach to these problems. The late Mo Mowlem, also a drugs minister in her time, declared similar views. We need more people with similar courage. There is some evidence to suggest that, at least in private, similar open-mindedness is gaining ground in Parliament.

Drug policy may be less good than it could be because it is usually formulated by those who do not know much about the subject. It is normally drafted by civil servants, most of whom are notably able, but it would be difficult to imagine a group of people less likely to know about the world of illicit drugs. Who does know in the round about all aspects of narcotic use? Certainly one could gather together a committee comprising addiction doctors, academics, lawyers, police officers, customs officials, journalists, teachers, probation officers and social workers, but even they would present an incomplete picture. The element missing, of course, is drug addicts themselves, both current users and those who have 'retired'. Without their honest and frank contributions it is unlikely that policy would be realistic or effective. Certainly, civil servants will have expert advice that they would call on: the Advisory Council on the Misuse of Drugs exists to give scientific advice to the government, but all too often policy documents give us little confidence that such a wide spectrum of experience has informed the drafting. There are almost certainly a few individuals who have a profound and wide knowledge of addiction, but whether they are known to the civil servants who draft policy is open to doubt. What is certain is that such a very difficult and intractable problem needs and deserves the very best policies that society can devise.

It is most unlikely that anybody over the age of forty will have a detailed or intimate knowledge of the way those who are in their twenties or thirties, live. To make good policy, it is necessary to understand how the young, among whom there will be many intermittent or recreational users of drugs, think. Drugs are a normal and almost universal part of life for this generation. Not all of them will or would take drugs, but they will not regard their friends who do so as deviant, nor will they pass any value judgements upon them. It is merely one of the many choices people make about life. Drugs are about as normal as going to the supermarket. This would not include the use of opiates, but it would include the smoking of cannabis, a snort or two of cocaine on a night out, an ecstasy tablet or two, and a number of other drugs, provided they are used in moderation. Young people accept that reasonable drug use happens and requires no comment. As the sociologists say, drugs have become 'normalized'.

Young people find it difficult to comprehend the world of their parents, and even more their grandparents, of which drugs were not a part, unless you include tobacco and alcohol. Some will say that drugs have taken the place of smoking and drinking, and that they will be the more healthy for it.

Those in middle life can only cross the divide by having an unusually close and frank relationship with their children and their friends. It may be asked if this all matters. It does matter if you are a civil servant involved in drafting drug policy. Unless you understand the 'normalness' of drug use, and that in most cases it is not even worthy of comment among the younger generation, the tone and substance of policy will be old-fashioned to those to whom it is directed, and will not command their respect. All too often in the past, addicts have read the latest policy statements, saying they 'don't know much about this' – and they were right.

Considerations of this kind lead one to wonder whether drug policy is either a subject which is given serious and expert attention, which it so clearly needs, or whether it is a Cinderella. After reading policy documents, an element of box-ticking about their production is quite apparent. A policy document has to be published on a certain pre-appointed day. Those responsible will be well-versed in the dark arts of departmental politics, and they will well understand the prevailing government thinking, and the extent to which their minister, who will present the document to Parliament, is prepared to push at the boundaries of current orthodoxy. This is likely to result in something bland and uncontroversial. The able civil servants concerned with drafting recognize that the problems of illegal drugs are so difficult that no public policy likely to command the approval of Parliament and public opinion would stand any chance of making much difference. It will be competent and well written and full of admirable and incontrovertible objectives, but any proposed action will be a bit vague and difficult to implement as other practical issues get in the way.

Let us return for a moment to the first five-year National Drug Strategy which was presented to Parliament in April 1998.[48] We have already noted how difficult it is to get evidence to plan actions that meet socially desirable general targets. In 2002, some of these were altered and others added, and not for the only time. The new targets were that drug-related crime was to be reduced (measured by the proportion of offenders testing positive at arrest). Numbers in treatment were to increase by 55 per cent by 2004 and up to 100 per cent by 2008; there was to be an increase year-on-year in the proportions of users successfully sustaining or completing treatment programmes, while poppy cultivation in Afghanistan was to be reduced by 70 per cent within 5 years (i.e. by 2007) and eliminated within 10 years (by 2012).

The eradication of poppy growing, and the original pledge to protect communities from the effects of drugs, were formally abandoned as being unrealistic. The numbers of users in treatment target was met comfortably with time to spare, but is has transpired that 'successfully sustaining or completing' a course of treatment means staying on the books for eight weeks – an exceptionally modest target, which could not be expected to effect any substantial change in behaviour. Specific and measurable targets are hostage to fortune, yet objectives that cannot be quantified are much less effective, and hardly worth the paper they are written on.

If these suspicions are true, it is a sad reflection on the functioning of the political process in Britain. And yet, there are those in government departments who have new and more radical ideas, but, it seems, are suppressed by the weight of orthodoxy. The evidence that such people exist is usually brought to our attention by a leak to a newspaper. One such was a report from the Crime Reduction Review to the Home Office, which argued strongly that controlled availability of drugs would greatly increase the government's influence over 'the way substances are used than is currently possible.'

Drug policy in most countries has reached a state of stalemate. There are only so many ways in which the same tired and failed measures can be presented. We desperately need to change direction and re-energize the arguments. This requires vision and political courage. We saw it happen in Portugal since 2005, and from the Portuguese example the rest of the world has the advantage of being able to see that the Cassandras were wrong. Professor Alex Stevens, commenting on the fact that the Portuguese experience seriously challenged the argument that liberalization of drug policy would lead to increased numbers of users, recently wrote that Britain's drug policy will not improve until we are bold enough to make the experiment.[49] Now, more than ever before, we need someone to stick their head above the parapet despite the powerful pressures militating against this bold action. Many members of Parliament fear that de-selection might await those who are thought to be too radical or 'soft on drugs', unless they happen to have a constituency reason for taking an interest in such a dangerous subject. 'Soft on drugs' is, of course, perceived to be the same as being 'soft on crime'. Another example of double-think.

Drugs policy has been hobbled by doctrinaire and fixed beliefs derived from archaic notions about the evil and satanic power of drugs to destroy the fabric of society. There remains a sense of moral panic just below the surface of any discussion of the subject. This thinking has had its day. It is time to let in the light of evidence, and to apply the same intelligence and intellectual rigour to the subject of drugs as has always informed the formulation of education or social policy. It will require a great measure of courage.

4 The Abject Failure of Prohibition

When President Nixon announced his intention to mount an all out 'War on Drugs', he stated that its aim was to so restrict availability of drugs by seizure and by preventing importation, that the price would rise to a level where few would be able to afford them.

Narcotic drugs are produced in vast quantities and in many different countries. Producers expect, and indeed allow for, seizure by the forces of law and order. In the light of experience, seizure would have to amount to about 90 per cent of all the drugs entering or being grown in a particular country before it would have a sustained effect on the price, and hence availability, of drugs on the street. No nation has ever got anywhere near that figure, and it is vanishingly unlikely that they ever will. It is completely unrealistic to expect seizures to make any long-term difference to the availability of drugs on our streets. Understandably, the forces of law and order put much emphasis on the weight of their seizures, and how they go up (and down) year by year, but even they have to admit that there is little correlation with street prices. We shall return to the question of seizure later in this chapter with some facts and figures.

It is now all but four decades since President Nixon launched his 'War on Drugs'. A generation and a half is more than enough time for even the most myopic to see that its theoretical basis was flawed, and that all the measures put in place, which have cost hundreds of billions of dollars, have been a complete failure. Hundreds of thousands of non-violent citizens are mouldering their lives away in prison because they got caught doing something which they did not regard as a crime against society, while millions of their fellow citizens continue to do the same, except that they have not been caught. A recent survey by the World Health Organization of seventeen countries found that America has the highest levels of use of cocaine and marijuana of any nation.[50] This finding, together with the fact that America has the most draconian and harsh drugs laws, proves beyond reasonable doubt that you cannot threaten or punish people into desisting from a behaviour which they enjoy, and do not regard as being harmful to society at large. Nobody can now say that this is not proven on the grounds that not enough time has elapsed. The American version of prohibition has failed irredeemably, and the nations of the world must summon up the courage to try something different.

Let us review the objectives on which the policy of prohibition is based. First, it is intended to reduce the availability of drugs. In the event, it has presided over a spectacular increase in drug production, availability and drug taking, while prices have fallen. The harm to health due to drugs has risen, and the social harms consequent upon criminal and illegal markets have become ever more worrying.

The second purpose is to reduce use by being an effective deterrent. Central to this was the belief that the criminal law acts in such a way. The proponents of prohibition never even try to offer any evidence that it works, because all the evidence points in the other direction. We will now look at some of it.

Day-to-day street prices are determined by supply and demand. This is the overwhelming price determinant, as it is with any commodity in a free or unregulated market. It is, therefore, by far the best indication of any shortage of supply. Internationally, there have only been two occasions on which drugs became scarce over a sustained period, and neither was due to successful law enforcement. The first was during the Second World War, where in America numbers of users fell dramatically because there was no legal source of supply and the criminal gangs were not in business. The second period was in the 1970s when there was a prolonged drought in South East Asia, the predominant producer of heroin at that time. Criminal suppliers were certainly in business, but they had no raw opium to process and distribute.

Other circumstances can influence price: crop failure, intense local police vigilance, or a re-organization of the local distribution network. But these result only in short term changes. Police and customs activity can have an impact on the street price of drugs: this happens, and while the rises can be steep, they are local and relatively short-lived until the criminal distributors reorganize their operations.

Globally, however, there are three other important influences. There is evidence of separate regional markets with quite different prices, largely because they do not trade with each other. For example, heroin from Myanmar (Burma) is five times more expensive than Afghan heroin; the same drug from Colombia is fifteen times as expensive as from Afghanistan. A second major price determinant is the distance of the market from the production source, reflecting the dangers of getting arrested crossing borders, and the attrition due to seizures. For example, Afghan heroin costing $2,400 per kilo at source will sell for $10,000 in Turkey and for an average of $44,300 in Western and Central Europe. Heroin from Colombia sells for $45,000 to $70,000 in the United States, and $119,000 in Canada, reflecting the dangers of trafficking the drug through the US. Lastly, to get a true basis for comparison of prices over time, allowances must be made for variations in currency values, inflation and purity of product.

There has been a steady and spectacular reduction in the price of street heroin in Britain over the past twenty-five years. The price paid in 1984 was between £90 and £100 per gram. The same gram, adjusted for purity, cost just under £30 in 2004.[51] Similar falls have been seen in the price of cocaine.

From January 2006 to the beginning of 2009, there was a continuing slow decline in both the wholesale and retail prices of heroin. Since 2009, prices have remained steady. In 2006 there was a fall in Britain, followed by unchanged prices. Cocaine prices in Europe have reflected the rate of seizure, which peaked in 2006.

Since then they have fallen. Cannabis prices do vary in different markets, and are notably high in Japan, which imports most of its requirements from Canada, South Africa and Holland, and in Russia. UK street prices have fallen substantially in the past three years, and do bear a close relationship to total European seizures. Adjusted for purity and inflation, street cannabis costs a little less than it did in 2002.

These prices cannot give much succour to the authorities who are spending hundreds of millions of pounds endeavouring to deny access to millions of users to a supply of drugs. The impact of government activity, though discernable, is insufficient to make users think hard about their habits. If prohibition worked there would be no alternative.

Drugs availability will also have an effect on the number of users. It will also be reflected in the acreage devoted to growing poppies and coca.

We will start by examining numbers of drug users to see if there have been any consistent changes in recent years which might be the consequence of prohibition. We need to be cautious when talking about the numbers of drug users. It is not feasible to count them. Even if careful and statistically sound sampling techniques are employed, accuracy depends on those sampled telling the truth. It also depends, crucially, on asking the right people.

In Britain, annual estimates of drug users are published, derived from the yearly British Crime Survey. A brief description of this will illustrate the difficulties and likely sources of error. The survey is based on questionnaires answered by members of a large and statistically valid number of households. Although questions about drug use are not answered face-to-face, and are recorded in private on a computer, there is always the possibility that the replies will not be true. Some may not wish to admit to potentially criminal behaviour. Although this is probably not a very major source of error, it will always tend to underestimate the number of users. Another minor problem is unreliable responders. The Survey includes a non-existent drug (Semeron) in the list about which it asks questions, and small numbers of people always claim that they have taken it. They are excluded from the analysis.

A much bigger problem arises because the questionnaire is only answered by those members of the household present when the surveyor calls, automatically excluding those at university or in residential education, training or rehabilitation, or those who are simply not in at the time. It also, very importantly, excludes those in prison, the homeless, and the armed forces. While the military may not be expected to have many drug takers, the other categories are all those among whom one would expect to find very significant numbers of drug users, and this leads to important under-reporting.

For example, the 2001 Survey[52] provided a figure for heroin users less than the number of heroin addicts presenting for treatment that year. And we know that there are always larger numbers of addicts who have not made any contact with treatment centres. This, collectively, is certain to result in significant underestimates of drug use, and there are other reasons to believe that this is true. Figures published in the 2009/10 British Crime Survey report that 29,000 sixteen to fifty-nine-year olds had taken heroin in the last month, and that 35,000 had used crack cocaine.[53] These findings should be set against the figure of problematic drug users, defined as those who take heroin and/or crack cocaine, of 320,000.[54] This estimate was arrived at by a quite different, and more accurate, method.

What can be said with reasonable confidence is that inaccuracies are likely to be similar every year, so trends are likely to be valid. There are more sophisticated and accurate ways of counting numbers in much smaller populations, but they are very time-consuming and hence expensive, and therefore not feasible in population surveys. These structural difficulties will exist in every country, and while some methods are likely to be better than others, none will ever be as accurate as, for example, the number of deaths in a particular community, or the total population from drug abuse.

It is a reasonable general presumption that in Britain today, and in most other countries, anyone who wants to use drugs can get hold of them. The overall figures in the most recent 2009/10 Survey of drug use tend to support this proposition.[55] Over the last ten years, the number of opiate users has been steady or declined a little. Ecstasy use has been very similar year-on-year since 2000. The use of hallucinogens has declined slightly, as have amphetamines. By contrast, the use of cocaine, either powder or crack, has become more popular.

The number of respondents reporting the use of cannabis in the past year was 6.6 per cent of the population, which amounts to 2.2 million people. This, however, represents a significant fall since the high point of over 11 per cent in 2003/4. The 2009/10 Survey[56] reported that over 40 per cent of the 16 to 24-year olds had taken illegal drugs at some time, and that 11.6 per cent of this group had used them in the past month – usually taken as a proxy measurement of current use.

These figures tell us how normal drug use is among young people, and how little attention they pay to the 'messages' which politicians are so keen to send them. Many of the thirty-something-year olds of today drink little alcohol, but they do take recreational drugs at the weekends, and regard this as quite normal behaviour. The contrary and random movements in the popularity of different drugs over time argues strongly that they are subject to fashion and personal choice rather than by any prolonged constraint on their availability. Plainly, if President Nixon's premise that the consequence of prohibition would be to choke off the number of users were true, there would be fewer drug takers than in the past. This is manifestly not the case.

Choice of which drugs to take appears to be not only subject to fashion, but to what is easily available. Recreational drug users may be quite fickle in their tastes. Most just want to be 'high', and, within limits, will use whatever is around. In the last year or two there has been a marked trend towards low quality, cheap and easily available drugs, which are being sold to a much less discerning group of customers than used to be the case. Whether this is a response to the economic climate of the moment, or it is a random change, is difficult to say, but it is not an altogether welcome change because it encourages poly-drug use. The taking of a cocktail of drugs, especially by the inexperienced, is dangerous, particularly when combined with alcohol.

While there have been some solid successes in seizures of cocaine in particular, it seems that the lower purities on the streets is more a function of the greed of dealers, than of a sustained shortage of their raw materials. Drugs of dubious quality and strength are bought off the Internet, and taken in combination with some of the 'legal highs' like mephedrone, though this has recently been made illegal.[57] The very recently published figures for 2010-11 show that mephadrone, or 'meow-meow', had become very popular with young drug takers.[58] It will be interesting to see if its new illegal status makes any difference to this.

Ketamine is enjoying a vogue, particularly among teenagers, because it is cheaper than cocaine and it gives a better 'high' than most pills. The black market is changing at the moment, but not for the first time, and almost certainly not for the last time. It is still doing a roaring business, and there is not a hint that prohibition is threatening its existence, or that it has had any major effect. That is not to say that there are not droughts of certain drugs from time to time. At the time of writing, heroin is difficult to find and of very poor quality, but the cause of this is purely speculative at present, and there are signs that it will be short-lived.

The United Nations Office on Drugs and Crime (UNCODC) 2010 annual World Drug Report does not make encouraging reading.[59] There has been some reduction in the area under poppy cultivation (consequently in global opium production), and some smaller reductions in cocaine cultivation and production, but there is not much other good news.

The best estimates of global drug use suggest that there are between 11 and 21 million people who inject drugs, and 16 to 38 million 'problem drug users'. The number of people who have used an illegal drug in the past year is believed to be between 155 and 250 million, or between 3.5 per cent and 5.7 per cent of the world population. Of course, many of these people will only have taken a drug once or twice, but most will have been more dedicated users, and the numbers are unimaginably large. Anybody who seriously believes that such huge numbers of people can be persuaded or bludgeoned into becoming abstinent is surely inhabiting another planet, yet the United Nations has committed its member states once more to ensure that overall drug supply and demand be 'eliminated or significantly reduced' by 2019. The Executive Summary of the report is cautious and circumspect about the chances of meeting this target, but one wonders why anyone would sign up to such an absurdly ambitious and unrealistic goal.

These figures provide no shred of evidence that prohibition has succeeded in reducing the numbers of drug users. We will now look at the important question of illegal drug production.

Since 1998, global potential opium production has increased by 78 per cent.[60] This is not a reflection of the consumption of opium products, and there is evidence to suggest that much of the recent output is being stockpiled. The figures for potential cocaine production are more modest at a 5 per cent increase, which has been reversed in the past year or so. Nevertheless, these figures can give no comfort to prohibitionists. Comparable figures for cannabis, ecstasy and other amphetamine-like drugs are extremely difficult to obtain because production is so decentralized.

Afghanistan is the source of most of the world's illicit opiates at the present time. In 2009, this country produced 89 per cent of global output, while Myanmar (Burma) contributed 4.8 per cent and Mexico 4.7 per cent. Production has declined in the past three years to 7,754 tonnes, but this remains substantially in excess of the total global demand – consumption and seizures – of about 5,000 tonnes per year.[61] Opium output is subject to occasional variations due to natural disasters, like drought or blight. Recently there has been a very sharp rise in the price of acetic anhydride, the key chemical with which raw opium is treated to turn it into heroin. A litre now costs $350-400. It is reported that it is common to see litre cans of this chemical carried as hand luggage on internal flights in northern Pakistan. Much attention is now being paid to cutting off the supply of precursor chemicals, and it looks as if this may be paying some dividends.

In 2008, a slight fall in cocaine production was accounted for by a significant decrease in Colombia, not quite offset by increases in Peru and Bolivia. Colombian production represents about 43 per cent of global output, while Peru contributes 38 per cent and Bolivia 19 per cent.[62] Crop eradication has been responsible for the fall in Colombian cocaine production. The US and European markets are now worth $37 and $43 billion respectively, while the total world market for cocaine is thought to be about $88 billion.[63] In the past twenty-five years the number of Americans using cocaine has halved, while the number of Europeans using it has doubled. This is probably because efforts to prevent Colombian cocaine reaching the American market have been increasingly successful, resulting in shortages met by decreasing the purity rather than increasing the price (although the purity-adjusted price has risen markedly). It seems that the new product has less appeal.

In Europe, the market for cocaine is headed by the United Kingdom, followed by Spain, Italy, Germany and France.[64] Both the UK and Spain have a higher prevalence of use than America. Although European street prices have halved in the last ten years, purity has declined and the dollar has weakened, so that the purity-adjusted price of cocaine in Europe has increased since 2002.

It is much more difficult to get reliable estimates of cannabis production because it is consumed almost all over the world, and grown locally. Herbal cannabis today includes the relatively weak preparation of leaves, and 'skunk', which is strong, and composed almost entirely of the flowers of the female plant. It is now grown indoors in very well lit rooms in Europe, Australia and the United

States. Hydroponic culture means that the plants are grown in water, to which a carefully calculated quantity of chemicals and nutrients is added. In Britain, this is undertaken on a large scale by Vietnamese criminal gangs, generating huge profits. It is also grown in cupboards, cellars and garden sheds by enthusiasts for their own use. Cannabis resin is produced in Morocco and Afghanistan, but it appears to be losing out to the hydroponically cultivated 'skunk' in many markets. Cannabis use is declining slowly in most western markets, though prices of high quality herbal 'skunk' have, if anything, risen a little.

There is a group of chemically produced stimulant drugs, sometimes lumped together as ATS, or amphetamine type stimulants, of which amphetamine, methylamphetamine and ecstasy-like drugs are the most important. They are usually manufactured close to the markets into which they are sold. Ecstasy started life in the dance and rave scene in Britain, but is now widely found. Methylamphetamine – 'crystal meth' or 'ice' – is a particularly nasty drug widely used in the Far East, North America and Australasia, which, so far, has made little impact in Britain. Amphetamine is popular in the Middle East, but has declined in popularity in Britain recently. While markets have changed (as they always do) there is certainly no evidence of a consistent fall in the production of drugs over the past five to ten years. Overall, the trend is probably towards an increase, and there is no discernable evidence that prohibition has cut production.

We will now return to the question of seizures. It was President Nixon's belief that confiscation and interdiction would be the means by which the market price of drugs would be driven up. This has simply not happened. Seizures, though very significant, are nowhere near great enough to have this effect on a global scale. They are regarded as a 'business expense' of the drug trade, and due allowance is made for it. Indeed, the Prime Minister's Strategy Group Report in 2003 concluded that seizures on a scale which could have a permanent effect on global prices was 'unattainable'.[65]

Both heroin and cocaine have long supply lines, and pass through many countries to reach their markets. In the case of heroin, there are two main routes by which it travels. Western Europe, which takes 37 per cent of Afghan heroin production, is supplied via the Balkans, which crosses Iran (in some cases through Pakistan), Turkey and the countries of South Eastern Europe. It is in Iran and Turkey that the majority of seizures are made – more than half the quantity impounded throughout the world. Serbia, Croatia, Slovenia, Austria, Albania, Hungary, Macedonia, Bosnia and Montenegro all make their contributions (in descending order) of the amounts confiscated. In 2008, a total of 7.6 tonnes were seized in Europe, 18 per cent in Britain, 14 per cent in Italy and 13 per cent in Bulgaria.[66]

The Northern route carries about 28 per cent of Afghan heroin output into the Russian Federation. It usually goes via Tajikistan, Kyrgyzstan and Kazakhstan, to supply the needs of an estimated 1.7 million addicts, who are notable for an alarmingly high HIV prevalence at 37 per cent of their overall population. Seizures along this route are very small.

A third supply chain, taking about 40 per cent of the Afghan production, is into Pakistan from whence, as mentioned before, large quantities go into Iran on their way to Western Europe. Smaller amounts are shipped to Asia, Africa and the United Arab Emirates, reaching China and East Africa: and by sea or air to the United Kingdom and Holland. Some heroin is, of course, consumed in Pakistan and there is a steady but unspectacular attrition by seizures along all these routes.

Substantial amounts of Afghan opium is not converted into heroin. About a quarter of this is trafficked in to Iran, where its use has been a traditional part of life for centuries. The rest is used in Afghanistan, Pakistan, India and the Russian Federation.

Global seizures of both heroin and opium continue to increase, while morphine confiscation has declined since 2008. It may well be that opium seizures have increased recently because of success by the authorities in denying access to the precursor chemicals. In 2008, the latest year for which figures are available, seizures of heroin and opium were at record levels.[67] Nevertheless, recent prices for street heroin in Western Europe are as low as they have ever been, though there has been a reduction in purity. Some of the losses will be by theft by other criminal organizations, and it is probable that about 80 per cent more heroin or cocaine is shipped from the producer country than the end market consumes.

Cocaine trafficking patterns and routes have changed in recent years in response to altered patterns of consumption. As noted, American demand for cocaine has been in decline for the past ten years or more. Cocaine bound for Western Europe, which is currently a growing market, comes from Colombia, but has a greater contribution from Peru and Bolivia than that which goes north to the US. Most of the cocaine bound for Europe is trafficked by sea via Spain and Holland, and to a lesser extent via West African states, though this route appears less used now.

Global cocaine seizures rose steadily until 2005 but have tended to level off since peaking at 70.5 tonnes.[68] Most seizures were made in South America (including Central America and the Caribbean), North America and Europe, in descending order.

Cannabis seizures have increased over the past fifteen years steadily, but fell after a peak in 2004. Since then they have again increased and reached a record level of about 6,600 tonnes in 2008. These are mainly achieved in North and South America and Africa, with Europe making a smaller contribution.

Worldwide seizures of the amphetamine-type stimulants have also increased steadily since 1996, and now amount to over 50 tonnes a year. The majority are amphetamines, with a very substantial contribution by methylamphetamine, and a smaller amount of ecstasy. Methylamphetamine is produced in mostly small illicit laboratories that play a constant cat and mouse game with the authorities.

This survey of recent trends in the markets of the most important drugs does not give any indication that the illegal drug trade is an industry staggering under the cosh of prohibition. On the contrary, it much more resembles a very well-run international business, quick to recognize the changes in its markets, and able to take skilful action to accommodate these changes. Furthermore, it is a business that is not subject to any bureaucracy, is not constrained by any laws, and pays no tax. The forces of law and order do have their successes, but their impact is mostly local and short-lived, and in some parts of the world they have to face the most murderous violence, as well as bribery and corruption. The drug business is a many-headed hydra – cut off one head and two others grown in its place. Underlying it all is the lure of riches beyond the dreams of avarice.

Violence is not one of the most obvious consequences of illegal drug taking, but it is there, lurking in the background. The use of some drugs can cause violent behaviour in certain circumstances. Crack cocaine comes most readily to mind, but violence is not a common feature of drug use. Ironically, violence is a very frequent concomitant of the use of the most common mind-altering drug – alcohol. This is, of course, completely legal, and widely abused. It leads to domestic violence, and yobbish and antisocial behaviour on a major scale. Our town centres bear witness to this every Saturday night, and it is not now confined to men. Binge-drinking young girls pose both a social nuisance and a threat to their own health. But these problems pale into insignificance compared to the ghastly range of criminal and murderous violence accompanying the production and trafficking of illegal drugs on the international stage.

If drugs are illegal, they are, by definition, the concern of organized criminals. Drugs are also the source of astronomic sums of money, which can match the Gross Domestic Product of some nation states. These drugs are so profitable because they are illegal, and the risks involved in dealing with them are extremely well rewarded. Drugs are not expensive to produce, and the profits to be earned are almost unimaginable.

Both heroin and cocaine require large acreages to grow, and are labour-intensive to harvest. It is no surprise, therefore, that they originate in countries where central government has tenuous control over some of its territory and struggles to maintain its authority. These conditions apply in Afghanistan, Myanmar (Burma), Colombia, Bolivia and Peru, among others, where circumstances also favour the growth of guerrilla armies. They find common cause with local farmers and protect them from any attempts by central government forces to interfere with their illegal agricultural activities. In exchange, the guerrillas demand highly profitable trading rights to finance their activities and pay for weapons. They in turn trade with armed criminal organizations engaged in refining or transforming the drugs as well as 'taxing' the cultivation and movement of the raw opium and coca leaves.

Criminal drug trafficking organizations make such huge profits that they will go to any lengths to further their ends. In South America and Mexico they have come to be known as 'cartels' whose members are usually recruited from the poor and deprived. Cartels offer a means for the underclass of local communities, whose culture they celebrate, to acquire power and money. In some cases, Mexican cartels draw inspiration from syncretic folk Catholicism, presided over by the Virgin of Guadalupe. Their activities will usually involve either violent confrontation with the governments of transit countries, or usurping the government altogether by means of high-level corruption. Strong or democratic governments have to be confronted, but weak or autocratic regimes can be suborned. This latter is the traffickers' preference because it allows them to get on with their business without interference and the losses involved in outright confrontation with the forces of law and order.

Paradoxically, efforts to stop trafficking by stable democratic governments can increase the level of violence. The criminals mark out their own territory or 'turf': in Mexico the cartels call it their 'plaza' – the place where drugs can most easily cross the border into America. Dislodging the gangs often means that the state has to employ the military, because the armed forces are both better equipped than the civilian police for such work and usually less corrupt. This can be a risky strategy in a democratically legitimate country. Slow progress in the fight against the gangs can be frustrating. The task is, in effect, to reclaim their own territory. And, if the criminal justice apparatus is ineffective, there will be a temptation to commit extra-judicial executions for their own protection. Similarly, civilian patrols or citizen-funded vigilante groups can turn into protection rackets, and, in the worst cases, into predatory paramilitary gangs which central government must control. Meanwhile, support for government by its citizens will leak away.

At the present time, about 200 tonnes of cocaine cross the US-Mexican border every year. The border stretches more than 2,000 miles, and although heavily patrolled and protected, still leaks like a sieve. From this activity, Mexican cartels make about $6 billion annually – more than enough to bribe whomsoever they want, and to equip themselves with weapons that are a match for anything used against them.

The Mexican cartels are now under pressure. Their income is falling, thanks to successful operations in which some 40,000 members, including the heads of a number of organizations, have been arrested in recent years. One hundred and seven criminals, including some very senior figures, have been extradited to America. This has led to waves of violence as those remaining try to capture the most profitable routes, and take advantage of rivals' weakness, or absence.

The cost to Mexico, as elsewhere, has been an escalation of violence. In the last three years, there have been more than 23,000 murders as ever more desperate criminals fight it out. And all the while, their other criminal and money-making activities like kidnapping, torture, extortion and human trafficking, continue unabated. President Felipe Calderon committed himself to ridding the country of these criminals when he took office five years ago, but he concedes that there is no end in sight to the violence. He sees no other option but to fight it out. Mexico is a rich country, but this is a high-risk strategy and he may not be able to carry his citizens with him.

The scale and bestiality of the violence and carnage is difficult to grasp. In September 2006, twenty-nine masked men burst into a discotheque in Morelia and bowled five decapitated human heads across the floor, accompanied by a bizarre statement of that particular cartel's assassination policy. In December 2009, a unit of Mexican special forces killed one of the bosses of the powerful Beltrán Leyva cartel. During this attack a young naval officer was killed. He was buried with full naval honours, and a day later cartel members burst into the grieving family's house and killed his mother, sister, brother and an aunt. The body of a thirty-six-year old man who had been abducted in one town, turned up in another, but his torso was in one place, his severed arms and legs in another, and his skull elsewhere. But his face had been flayed, and turned up sewn to a football. And to soften up prisoners and make them talk, 'bone tickling' was used which involved putting an ice-pick through the skin and dragging it up and down the underlying bone.

And there is the grizzly lexicon of mutilation by which even the dead can speak. Cutting out the tongue means that 'he talked.' A finger removed and put in the mouth or up the rectum means that he betrayed his clan. Castration indicates that he paid too much attention to someone else's woman. A severed arm tells you that he stole from his consignment of drugs, and removal of a leg that he tried to walk away from the cartel. Decapitation is a simple statement of power, and a warning. But it is the day-to-day ordinariness, the routinization of torture, mutilation and death, which is so chilling. It has lost its power to shock, and has become as normal as eating a meal.

Do not believe that this satanic vision does not concern us simply because it is half a world away. Home-grown violence among and between gangs who import and distribute heroin and cocaine in Britain does not have much to learn from the Mexicans. Turks and Pakistanis, who deal in heroin, and the Vietnamese, who grow cannabis on an industrial scale up and down the land, settle their arguments by direct and calculated violence. Drug deals are sometimes paid in guns, and the drug business is directly responsible for the upsurge of gun crime in some of our big cities. A recent Home Office report concluded that: '[Illegal] drug markets appear to ... represent the single most important theme in relation to the illegal use of firearms, characterized by systemic violence that appears to increase towards the street (retail) end of the market. Firearms possession was reported in relation to robberies of drug dealers (that appear to be increasing), territorial disputes, personal protection and sanctioning of drug market participants.'[69]

Perhaps rightly we pride ourselves in Britain on our relative freedom from corruption. It surely exists, and always will, but it is not woven into the fabric of life as it is in some parts of the world. But from time to time we read of a corrupt policeman being arrested, and it is often drugs which are at the bottom of it. It is money that corrupts, and the easiest source of money in the world is dealing in narcotic drugs. It is risky, but the rewards are so huge that many are tempted, and quite a few succumb. As the saying goes, 'everyone has his price'.

Institutionalized corruption produces a nightmare society in which you can trust nobody – even the highest in the land – and you must be suspicious of everybody. President Calderón in Mexico is conducting his battle against the cartels in this hellish situation. Time and time again the most senior and most trusted officials, police chiefs and military commanders prove to be dishonest and in the pay of the cartels, to whom they betray the secret plans of the authorities. It is not possible to rely on even the most elite and hand-picked special forces, significant numbers of whom have defected to the cartels and become the trainers of their private armies.

Corruption on such a scale and degree of penetration threatens the very existence of a democratic country. Fortunately Mexico is a well-off and a well-organized society, and the cartels operate in reasonably well-defined areas, but there are many states in the world which lack the institutions and maturity to resist the onslaught of drug money, which may tip them into chaos and ungovernability. Such failed states then become a responsibility and a drain on the international community.

We must accept that trafficking in illegal drugs, with the spectacular amounts of money it generates, is a major, if not the major, cause of violence and corruption in our modern world. Of course, there are other corrupting influences, and corruption will always be, to varying degrees, a feature of all societies. The violence associated with the drug smuggling business is a measure of the amount of money it makes, and the desperation with which criminals will fight. But it is not the drugs themselves that have a large intrinsic value, it is their illegality which earns the money. The policy of prohibition must directly bear the responsibility for handing such a gigantic industry to criminals, who are polluting the world in which we live by their outrageous behaviour, far beyond the limits of tolerability. In this sense it can be said that prohibition has not just failed, but that it has positively, directly and predictably perverted our world and has made it a much less safe and pleasant place in which to live.

There is another wholly undesirable feature of the illegal status of drugs which prohibition confers. Drug taking is overwhelmingly a habit of the young, and the young are impressionable, and go through quite a normal stage of rebellion. Anything illegal has, therefore, a certain cachet or attraction. Drug taking is 'cool'. It is a secret and defiant act that will earn the disapproval of your parents and other authority figures. It carries a whiff of danger, and exposes you to the influence of older friends, who may appear quite sophisticated when they suggest that you try something because it is illicit. It is a universal truth that forbidden fruit is always the sweeter.

There can be few children who do not try to smoke a cigarette, and usually a little later, try a drink of alcohol. Regarded as a normal part of growing up, and, since both are legal, it occasions little comment. It might even be the subject of a sensible conversation about the perils and pleasures of tobacco and alcohol, which would be worthwhile. This is not so easy in the case of trying a drug unless, of course, the drug had been made legal, in which case such a discussion could join the other things, like sex, which have to be the subject of honest dialogue with parents as part of growing up. It is a mistake to underestimate the glamour conferred on drugs by their illegality.

The fact that drugs are illegal is used, certainly in America, as an excuse for the erosion of civil liberties. The 'War on Drugs' has militarized the police and resulted in the use of more unjustified and excessive force in situations when drugs are not involved, as well as when they are. Arming the police further, raises the risks of inappropriate use of weapons.

Billions of dollars are committed to the 'War on Drugs', spawning enforcement agencies which are huge and difficult to keep accountable. The Drug Enforcement Administration, the CIA, the FBI and the new Department of Homeland Security together employ over 250,000 people and cost something close to $100 billion a year. The clear connection between drugs and international terrorism increases the possibility of the inappropriate use of force and other powers, sometimes backed by constitutional amendments. This is likely to grow insidiously, often against those least able to defend themselves. And the limitless amount of money generated by drug trafficking makes it inevitable that some police officers and other enforcement agents will become corrupted. It seems that society has sanctioned unacceptable and intolerable behaviour by the authorities in the name of 'defeating the scourge of drugs'.

Such high-handed and even criminal action is not confined to 'the authorities'. For example, commercial or quasi-charitable organizations have sprung up that claim to treat 'chemical dependence'. One such, known as Straight Inc., operated throughout the 1980s until it was closed down in 1993, turning out to be little more than a brain-washing movement coercing its victims into 'treatment', and holding them there against their will. It collapsed in a welter of legal judgements for false imprisonment and other crimes, and many awards of substantial damages. No doubt such institutions were started by well-meaning people. Straight was much praised by the Reagans, but its methods were unacceptable.

All this springs from a peculiarly American belief that if right-minded people mobilize in sufficient numbers they will prevail upon their temporarily deluded young people. They have no knowledge of the reasons why some should be so wayward.

There are many innocent victims of prohibition's traditionally aggressive stance. Thousands of US servicemen have been dismissed from the military for producing a compulsory urine sample which tested positive for a drug. Such tests are not infallible, nor are they always interpreted correctly, as two young Navy doctors proved. Their tests suggested that they had used opiates, and they were ignominiously discharged from the Navy. But they were determined to clear their names, and to be reinstated. The culprit turned out to be poppy seeds on the bagels in the hospital canteen.

In the past year or two, another challenge to the authorities has emerged as a major problem. For some years there have been a growing group of drugs with mind-altering properties, which became known as 'legal highs'. They are legal to use simply because the authorities have not made them illegal, because it takes time to gather information on the actions of each and every one. They are all man-made drugs, and many are chemically related. The best known are BZP (Benzylpiperazine), which enjoyed popularity in New Zealand in the early 2000s, and the until recently legal, mephadrone (also known as 'meow-meow' or 'MCAT'). Many have fanciful street-names like 'Ivory Wave', 'Spice' or 'Benzo Fury', presenting a growing problem to the regulatory bodies.

Most of the new drugs come from China, and the scale of the problem promises to be overwhelming. In 1950 there were twenty such drugs, and by 2000 the number had risen to two hundred, the subject of a recent report addresses the difficulties.[70] While rehearsing the various options for control, it recognizes there will be too much application of the 'precautionary principle'. By this they mean that there will always be pressure to ban or make something illegal, both as a matter of public safety, and because it will be impossible to gather all the information on which to base a more considered judgement in a timely fashion. It also acknowledges that this approach will almost certainly result in making a few drugs illegal, which might otherwise be 'useful' as a less damaging alternative to some of the drugs in common usage. The authors recognize, of course, that proscribing any drug does not stop its use – it merely makes it more expensive.

This is yet another example of the ultimate folly of seeking to control the availability of drugs effectively. The ingenuity of chemists, allied with the inextinguishable appetite of so many for their products, will guarantee that the authorities will never be in effective control.

5   Drugs and Crime

Nothing in the world of illegal drugs is straightforward. It is commonly said that a large proportion of acquisitive crime is drug-related, and this is almost certainly true. But which comes first – the criminality or the drugs – is a complex question. So, too, is the concept of illegality.

In the present state of the law in Britain, possessing any illegal drug is a criminal act, but the use of a drug is not. In this strict sense, everybody who takes any illegal drug is a criminal because you cannot take a drug without first possessing it. The unlikely exception would be if the taker were to be fed the drug by another who possessed it, which can occur when someone's drink or food is 'spiked' as either a prank or in order to render the person unconscious. However, we need to discuss principles, not technicalities.

In Britain, an illegal drug is one which appears on the ABC classification of the Misuse of Drugs Act 1971, or its subsequent amendments. The classification was intended to reflect the harm which could arise from the use of the drug, but in recent years there has been an ill-disguised tendency to allow politics, rather than evidence, to determine the classification. The Act, notably, does not mention either alcohol or tobacco. Any contravention of the Act is sometimes referred to as a 'drug offence'. It might be possession of a proscribed drug, but it also could be importing, exporting, producing, supplying, cultivating, or allowing these offences to be committed on your premises.

A drug-related crime is an offence which is caused, in some way, by drug use. Most commonly this is shoplifting, burglary, robbery or fraud, to pay for drugs. It can also include crimes committed by traffickers and dealers. The only importance of these distinctions is that they are sometimes used when writing about drugs and crime. Usually such offences are all collectively referred to as drug-related crime.

Yet the complexity of illegality cannot be stated so simply. First, nearly all the drugs forbidden by the 1971 Act have important or significant medicinal uses, and, when prescribed by a doctor, are legal. Indeed, modern surgery would not be possible without the uniquely effective pain-killing properties of the opiates. A little more confusingly, they are also legal when prescribed by a doctor as part of the treatment of an addict. *In other words it is not the drug that is illegal, but rather the reason for which it is used.* And the last thing to say about illegality is that the great majority of drug takers do not regard themselves as criminals because they do not believe that they are harming themselves or society, or that they are transgressing any principle of natural or social justice.

Of course, occasionally, they are wrong and do harm themselves or incur publicly funded expenditure, but in the vast majority of instances of drug taking, no harm is done. This fact is most important and insufficiently acknowledged. Whatever the popular conception, most people who take a forbidden drug are not, and do not see themselves as, criminals. They would not think of committing other crimes which have obvious and universally accepted reasons for being so described.

Laws which are seen by many as arbitrary, are not very effective. Of course, there are other drug users who have to admit to committing acquisitive crime, or to becoming dealers, to whom these remarks do not apply. And looming over this whole subject is the fact that there are distinguished minds who do not believe that the state has the right to deny its citizens the choice of whether to use a particular drug or not, provided that they are aware of, and prepared to accept, the consequences.

It is also worth considering that illegality plays a very significant part in the initiation of young impressionable people into drug taking. The use of illegal drugs is seen as rebellious, risky and anti-authority. But if they were legal they would be no more (or less) attractive than rock climbing. Both involve some measure of danger, but one is potentially harmful and socially damaging, and the other is positively healthy and socially constructive.

The relationship between crime and drugs is a very clear and important issue. It has been extensively studied, and the evidence is at times contradictory. We need to examine whether, and how often, using drugs leads to criminal behaviour, or if being inclined to criminal behaviour predisposes individuals to drug taking. There are three possibilities to explain the proposed association. The Reciprocal Theory would suggest that drug taking leads to crime, and that crime causes drug use – that it is a two-way relationship. The Common Cause model proposes that drug taking and criminal behaviour both have their origins in a common factor, such as, for example, social deprivation and exclusion. We know that the most disadvantaged are ten times more likely to become addicted than the less deprived. We also have evidence that delinquency, aggressive behaviour and family breakdown are more common in these poor areas.[71] These facts make the relationship between drugs and crime more complex than direct cause and effect.

That there is a strong link between drug use and criminality is a near-universal finding. Almost all studies come to the same conclusion. Drug takers are more likely to be involved in crime than the general population, and criminals are more likely than non-criminals to take drugs. But we need to know more, and it has not proved easy to tease out the dynamics of this relationship. There is excellent evidence that the drugs most often associated with crime are heroin and crack, and that the crimes most often related to drug use are shoplifting, general theft, drug dealing and prostitution (though the latter is not a crime).[72]

These findings are what would be expected, and at least there is evidence that they are true. Those who abuse multiple drugs (poly-drug users) resort to crime more often that those who use one drug, and users of a Class A drug in combination with others, commit more offences than those who only use combinations of recreational drugs. These, again, are expected findings, because the use of drug cocktails is a feature of the most chaotic phase of a drug-taker's career, when he or she is hell-bent on the pursuit of pleasure, to the total exclusion of rationality.

Studies have been done looking at the age at which drug taking and offending starts, and the results are interesting. The use of recreational drugs, mainly cannabis, precedes criminal behaviour, but the reverse is true when hard drugs are considered.[73] These are very consistent findings in the case of soft drugs, and fairly consistent in regard to Class A drugs. Studies following individuals over time show that offending is directly related to the quantity of drugs being consumed, and that crime rates fall away when an individual becomes abstinent.

Crimes committed during periods of heavy use are theft, confidence tricks and forgery, and drug dealing. It seems that heroin use is associated mainly with shoplifting, while crack users prefer fraud, handling stolen goods, and dealing. Furthermore, over half the property crime is committed in the poorest one fifth of our communities. Research based on interviewing drug users identifies a number of relevant factors. The economic necessity to fund a habit is paramount as an incentive to criminal behaviour – shoplifting, prostitution and drug dealing most commonly, and burglary much less so. There is also a considerable amount of theft by addicts from other addicts. Drugs or alcohol are taken by some criminals to give them the courage required to commit a burglary.[74]

Another view that has emerged is that drugs may amplify criminal tendencies, but not cause people to commit crimes they would otherwise not undertake. And lastly there is a suggestion that drug use can lead to crime by association. Drugs have to be purchased from dealers who are part of the criminal world, and it is possible that some may get drawn into that world as a consequence. When interviews are conducted with criminals, there is a group for whom the proceeds of crime fund their enjoyable drug use – they simply choose to spend their ill-gotten gains on drugs. One intriguing fact emerges from a consideration of drugs and crime.

It is always assumed that drug taking and criminal activity are positively related. In other words, using drugs increases criminality, and offending leads to drug use. There is some evidence that the reverse may be true – that in some circumstances the use of a drug may curb the urge or tendency to commit a criminal act. For example, smoking some heroin can reduce aggression to where there does not seem to be any point in committing such an act.

There is, lastly, a form of criminality associated with drug supply that is often overlooked. Drug trafficking is a highly sophisticated international criminal activity, and because it is so profitable those involved will stop at nothing to get their way. In the last few years, firearms have become common, particularly in the crack cocaine trade, and those who carry them are prepared to use them. Some dealers will also sell guns, and even accept them in payment for drugs. Violence is threatened or used to deter fraud, betrayal, theft and dishonesty. The scale and ubiquity of drug dealing in the big cities has spawned a gun culture which has spilled over into other forms of criminal activity, and is now a matter of serious concern, for innocent people are getting killed in cross-fire.

The 2006 Home Office report concluded that: 'Illegal drug markets appear to ... represent the single most important theme in relation to the illegal use of firearms, characterized by systemic violence that appears to increase towards the street (retail) end of the market. Firearms possession was reported in relation to robberies of drug dealers (that appear to be increasing), territorial disputes, personal protection and sanctioning of drug market participants.'[75] But at a more modest local level, turf wars break out as new suppliers try to muscle in on this lucrative trade. Obviously those aggrieved can have no recourse to law, so they settle their differences by violent and criminal means. The recent explosive rise in the number of cannabis farms, mainly run by Vietnamese criminal gangs, has brought its own brand of rough justice.

The finding that criminality precedes heroin and cocaine usage is puzzling at first, but it could be that, since Class A drugs are typically used at a slightly older age than cannabis, offending behaviour is related to the recreational drug taking which went before the heroin. It must be remembered that many drug users pay for their own pleasures, and never commit a crime except, of course, possessing the drug that they use. But others will resort more readily to shoplifting, and with little or no remorse.

There is, though, another possible explanation. All the studies discussed take as their raw material a group of individuals – either a population of drug takers, or of criminals. While there will be some overlap, it is a near-certainty that the two groups will be significantly different. In the criminal group will be some who have embarked upon a life of crime and reward themselves with a few lines of cocaine from time to time. These 'young lags', though they commit crimes and take drugs, are quite different from the heroin user 'who has no option' but to fund his habit by acquisitive crime. But we need not get too concerned whether criminality precedes or follows drug taking. The reality is that the most obvious and natural home for drugs in Western societies is in those communities that are already poor, marginalized and lacking in opportunities for self-betterment, and which are also breeding grounds of criminality. Both drug taking and criminal behaviour are choices which are independent of each other, though it will not seem that way to those obliged to try to create a life in the worst of our inner-city ghettos.

In the late 1980s, the government funded the National Treatment Outcome Research Study (NTORS) to look in detail at many aspects of drug treatment in a large population of British drug takers. In their report for 2000[76] they found that 1,075 heroin addicts had committed 27,000 acquisitive crimes in the three months before entering treatment, but that just 10 per cent of them were responsible between them for over 20,000 of the crimes. More than half had committed no crimes at all in the same period, and the rest engaged in desultory low-level theft. This is further evidence that many users of drugs are not criminals, except in the narrow sense that Parliament has dictated that anyone who possesses a drug is committing a crime.

The great majority of those who acknowledge a link between drugs and crime subscribe to the 'drugs cause crime' view, and that the necessity to get money to pay for them is overwhelmingly the most important reason why they enter the world of criminality. This is also the assumption underlying government policy, and treatment. However, there does not appear to be a correlation between overall crime rates in Britain and the prevalence of Class A drug usage. A lot of crime is in no way related to drug taking or dealing, and the non-problematic or recreational use of drugs is not associated with crime at all. This leads to the conclusion that it would be unwise to regard crime figures or trends as a direct indication of the success or failure of drug policy.

The important question of the total costs to society of illegal drugs, and who bears them, has been authoritatively studied by Professor Christine Godfrey and her colleagues at the Centre for Health Economics at York University. For the sake of simplicity, she confined her study to the economic and social costs of Class A drugs (overwhelmingly heroin and cocaine), in the year 2000. It is a most worthwhile piece of work, revealing some startling findings.[77] Certainly there are some methodological issues which may be controversial, and the figures have to be adjusted for inflation since 2000, but three main findings emerged which could probably not have been predicted.

The total costs, which are an aggregate, and other costs borne by individuals or by society at some time in the future, amounted to £12 billion a year. Of crucial importance is that 99.7 per cent of this sum was incurred by users of heroin and cocaine – usually known as 'problematic users'. Taking of all other drugs by non-problematic users, a much bigger group of people, only accounted for 0.3 per cent of the total costs. Furthermore, 88 per cent of the costs was incurred in criminal activities. It is sometimes said that shoplifting is a victimless crime. That this is not so is clearly shown by the aggregate victim cost of crime amounting to over £8 billion.[78] Put in another way, annual victim costs of crime committed by the problematic group of users averages some £31,000 per victim, which falls by two thirds to £11,000 when addicts enter a treatment programme. Herein lies the justification for expenditure on treatment, for society can be seen to make a 'profit' which far exceeds the cost of treatment.

Revised estimates for the year 2003-4 have been published, but according to revised methodologies.[79] While the two sets of figures are not strictly comparable, nevertheless, the estimated aggregate costs of money spent on the consequences of drug taking was £15.4 billion – a figure which would now be much greater, even without inflation.

The study also provided information about acquisitive crime, and its criminal justice and victim costs. Fraud, largely connected with credit cards, accounted for about half the victim costs at £4 billion, burglary £2.7 billion and robbery and shoplifting £1.6 billion each. These estimates did contain a notional sum for the human cost of being burgled or mugged, and the effects this may have had on employment and productivity.

To many people it comes as a shocking surprise that drug taking is rife in our prisons. But it should not be unexpected. Up to 80 per cent of all those entering some prisons test positive for opiates, irrespective of the nature of the crimes for which they have been sentenced. In 2005 it was estimated that there were about 39,000 problematic drug users in prison at any one time – roughly half the total prison population.[80] This is an enormous problem for the prison authorities. Until recently drug treatment in prison was primitive. In spite of fine words from the government, it is still very poor, and patchy.

Many inmates become addicted for the first time in prison, and there is an ambivalence on the part of prison staff towards drug use among the inmates. Drugs are extensively available in prison. They come over the wall in tennis balls and other missiles, they are brought in by visitors, and some prison officers sell them. There is a tolerance of their presence because it is felt that drugs curb aggression, and make prisoners more compliant and easier to deal with. As usual, any more effective policy would cost more public money, which is not likely to be forthcoming.

Most of the writing about drugs and crime has been done by academic criminologists. They naturally focus on the research literature, and their own work in the field, but it must be doubtful if they have much experience of talking to addicts and discussing these issues with them. In my own experience, drug users in treatment are very ready to talk about their past with frankness and honesty. A number of themes emerge from many such conversations. Firstly, large numbers of heroin users (but by no means all) have been involved in criminal activity, but mostly of low grade theft from parents or other family members, and perhaps some shoplifting. There are, or course, others who committed more serious or persistent acquisitive crime.

Second, in the great majority of cases, these activities were confined to the early and most chaotic phase of their drug taking. Thirdly, most are ashamed of what they did when they were in the most obsessive and driven stage of their relationship with drugs. Finally, quite a few of them have convictions for possession of drugs, but not for any acquisitive act. In other words their crime was technical only. There certainly are patients in addiction treatment who have convictions for drug dealing, for violence, or for more serious acquisitive crimes. Many have been in prison, but, again, the offences were committed early in their drug taking careers. These facts, collectively, tend to support the view that drug taking leads to crime, rather than the relationship being the other way round.

It can be argued that those in treatment represent a different population than those at an earlier and more criminally active stage of their drug taking, and that therefore the above remarks cannot be applied to them. Going into treatment voluntarily is a sign of growing maturity, and those who choose to do so are necessarily older than the hotheads who are not yet ready to make this decision. But that does not mean that the trajectory which both groups have, or will, follow through their addiction will be different. Neither addiction, nor the response of individuals to acquiring a habit, have changed over recent years, though perhaps the fickle winds of fashion may have influenced which drugs are taken. For these reasons it is likely that the above remarks are valid.

The practical importance of considering the inter-relationship of drugs and crime is to help us reach a robust conclusion about the likely effect that legalization of drugs would have on the incidence of different types of crime. One of the most commonly advanced arguments for legalization is that it would reduce criminality. It is difficult to avoid the conclusion that there would be a positive effect on shoplifting and property crime if drugs were legal and could be bought at a well-judged price. But some of the voices raised are very likely to be over optimistic.

If we are correct in believing that much acquisitive crime is committed by young addicts in the early stages of their relationship with heroin or crack cocaine, the reduction could be less than we might suppose. The behaviour of this group will not be ruled by the same logic as that of their older colleagues. The young are more impetuous and opportunistic, and so act on the spur of the moment without much thought. Although we must be careful to point out that decriminalization and legalization are crucially different, the experience from Portugal, which decriminalized the use and possession of all illegal drugs in 2001, may give some clues. In the early years there was an increase in opportunistic street crime, but a reduction in more complex, premeditated crimes, and those likely to involve threats of violence.[81]

How relevant this observation is to the case for legalization is difficult to say, because decriminalization does not allow regulated and legal markets for drugs, which are therefore still in the hands of criminals. Other findings, however, may be more relevant. The number of offences committed under the influence of drugs halved after decriminalization, and a lot of police time was saved, which could be devoted to more serious matters.

Common sense suggests strongly that there would be a fall in overall crime if drugs were legalized. To prove this is not possible without trying it out. Herein lies a major difficulty, and for many, a good reason to resist the policy. Sooner or later we will have to choose, for the present situation is increasingly untenable.

So far in this chapter we have been concerned with crimes committed in a domestic setting. Throughout the book there are many references to criminal activity on a much bigger stage. It is probably true to say that drugs fund the majority of serious international crime. Corruption of law enforcement agencies, senior military officers, politicians, customs officials and others is routine in countries through which drugs are trafficked, usually accompanied by obscene violence. As a result, small states with insecure institutions fail and descend into chaotic ungovernability. The rise of money laundering as an international problem is almost all attributable to the necessity to disguise illegal drug profits. And international terrorism, narco-terrorism, is largely funded by drug money .

Clearly, crimes committed against individuals or their property have a great impact, and collectively represent a major problem in any society. They also carry great cost, both monetary, and in terms of nuisance, misery and fear, making a society less pleasant to live in. These are bad enough problems, but pale into insignificance when compared to all the criminality, murder, violence, corruption and international terrorism funded by the illegal drug trade, which would itself not exist if drugs were a mere agricultural commodity, like coffee.

The answer to this terrible burgeoning problem is not prohibition. It has got steadily worse in spite of prohibition. And more of the same will only exacerbate the problem. What would make a major difference is to remove the profit from drugs trafficking. The only way to do that is to make drugs legal so that they can be bought and sold in a market very much like tobacco. It is an extraordinary and unique opportunity, but it depends on the international community taking a radical and far-sighted decision even though it will be opposed by many. It is difficult to be sanguine about the chances that it will ever happen.

6   Producer and Transit Countries

South America and Cocaine

Cocaine is a drug derived from the leaves of the plant Erythroxylon coca. It is a shrub or small tree, which grows exuberantly in the foothills of the Andes in Colombia, Peru, Ecuador and Bolivia. Its fresh leaves have been chewed by South Americans for thousands of years. The concentration of psychoactive ingredients is low in the leaves, so the effects are only of mild stimulation, which makes physical work easier. Coca was regarded by these peoples as a gift from God, and it soon acquired an important part in their religious ceremonies. During the fifteenth century, the Inca in Peru started to tend coca plantations, but there is no evidence that coca chewing had any corrosive effect on the societies that used it. Trouble started when the Europeans arrived.

Spanish and the Portuguese navigators and explorers of their day were in the service of Kings spurred on by dreams of the fabulous riches of El Dorado. In 1494, they signed, with papal blessing, the Treaty of Tordesillas, by which Spain was to get the territories to the west, and Portugal those to the east of a line which roughly divides modern Brazil in half. In about 1511, Vasco Nunez de Balboa, accompanied by Hernan Cortes, the future conqueror of Mexico, crossed the Isthmus of Panama and discovered the Pacific Ocean. Francisco Pizarro, who had sailed for the New World in 1502 in search of adventure and gold, heard travellers' tales of the great wealth of Peru. After two abortive expeditions and many difficulties, Pizarro returned to Spain with evidence of the existence of fabulous riches, and gained the support of King Charles V, by then the Holy Roman Emperor, for a new expedition. In 1532 Pizarro defeated the Inca chief Atahualpa, captured Cusco, destroyed the Inca Empire and founded a new capital at Lima. There, in 1535, he was killed by one of his lieutenants, with whose father he had quarrelled.

Meanwhile, by 1505, accounts of coca leaf use had been brought back to Spain by Amerigo Vespucci and others. Keen to exploit the new possibilities, the Spanish king made land grants to adventurers, who took over the Inca plantations, and at the same time changed the law to enable Spanish taxes to be paid in coca leaves. The Jesuit priests condemned coca chewing as the work of the devil, but they soon recognized that chewing did indeed give strength and energy, and that the habit was ineradicable. They turned defeat into victory by taking a tenth of the value of the coca crop as a tithe to support the Roman Catholic Church.

By 1545 the mines at Potosi had been discovered, which, in the subsequent fifty years produced half the world's output of silver. At an altitude of 14,000 feet, it was difficult to mine and to transport to the coast. Forced labour was introduced, and to keep the workforce happy and working hard, they were provided with plenty of coca leaves. Spain thus found a way of financing the production of silver with something that cost nothing. In 1577, Nicholas Monardes' text on coca was translated into English, and he returned to Europe with the leaves. They failed to excite any particular interest however, because unknown to him, active alkaloids in the leaves start to lose their potency as soon as they are picked.

The next two centuries witnessed the recognition that coca had obvious medicinal properties. In 1630, the Dutch captured Pernambuco (now Recife, Brazil) from whence they sent plants to the University of Leiden, which had a noted botanical garden. The development of coca as a medicine started with its inclusion in a Dutch Materia Medica of 1708 by a doctor and botanist, Boerhaave, who was in charge of the Leiden gardens, but he failed to show further enthusiasm, probably because he could not get adequate supplies of fresh leaves. Subsequently, coca was examined at the Museum of Natural History in Paris in 1750 by Linnaeus and Lamarck, and illustrated in Lamarck's encyclopaedia of 1786.

Sir William Hooker, the legendary botanist, at the time Director of Kew Gardens, wrote an illustrated scientific description of the coca plant in 1835 from a specimen sent from Peru. Coca was by then clearly going to have important medical applications. As a result, seeds were sent to Kew in 1869, where it was cultivated, and distributed to botanical research stations throughout the British Empire. Coca bushes grew well in Nigeria, Sierra Leon, Ceylon and on the tea estates of Assam, but they did not thrive in the Blue Mountains of Jamaica. It later emerged that the strain of coca grown in Java, of unknown provenance, grew leaves containing up to four times as much cocaine as those of South American origin.

A little later, coca tincture (an alcoholic solution) was used in throat surgery, the first application of its important function as a local anaesthetic. In the 1850s, cocaine – the active ingredient of coca leaves – was extracted and isolated by the German chemist Albert Niemann, who gave it its name. Shortly after, in 1862, the German pharmaceutical company, Merck, produced one hundred grams or so of pure cocaine hydrochloride.

In 1863, a Corsican pharmacist, working in Paris, launched his 'Vin Mariani' – red wine in which the alcohol had leached the cocaine out of the coca leaves. He was a brilliant publicist, and soon the great and the good of the western world were singing its praises. Its success may have been in part because, unknown to Mariani, cocaine breaks down to combine with alcohol in the body to produce cocaethylene, which is itself a reinforcing psychoactive substance. Its success soon attracted many competitors, but they were not so brilliantly promoted. But in due course, it did have a powerful rival.

John Pemberton, a chemist from Georgia who was gravely injured in the American Civil war, had fallen on hard times. He launched his 'French wine cola' in 1884. It contained red wine, kola nuts and coca leaves. To foil the anticipated attack from the Temperance movement, he removed the wine in 1886, and called his new product 'Coca-Cola'. In 1902 he made another crucial change by removing the coca leaves in response to outrageous racist claims that black Americans took cocaine before raping white women. It is an extraordinary irony that, without either of its active ingredients, Coca-Cola went on to become perhaps the most successful consumer product of all time.

Following the end of the Napoleonic wars, the pace of South American exploration quickened. Interesting ideas started to circulate. Mountaineers were convinced that chewing coca leaves made climbing Mont Blanc much easier. It was said by an Indian Army doctor that coca should be used for 'assuaging thirst during great exertion in hot countries', and an Austrian doctor showed that coca was capable of enhancing endurance. Finally, a Russian doctor proposed that cocaine might prove to be a useful anaesthetic.

The young Sigmund Freud was uncritically, and rather disgracefully, seduced by cocaine as a cure for morphine addiction. His idea came from a publication which proved to be an advertising vehicle for Parke-Davis, the producers of cocaine in America, who paid Freud to endorse their brand of the drug. He went on to elaborate a bizarre theory that it could be used to cure a whole range of common symptoms, for which there was no good evidence. He himself continued to use cocaine until about 1912.

It fell to Karl Koller, a friend of Freud's, to do the rigorous experiments to prove that cocaine was indeed a useful local anaesthetic. This announcement, in 1884, led to an explosion in its use, particularly in eye surgery. Merck's production of cocaine rose from less than a pound in 1884 to 158,352 lbs two years later. The American producer, Parke-Davis, sent a young chemist, Henry Rusby, to Bolivia, where he devised a method of making coca paste. This proved to have two great advantages over coca leaves: first, the cocaine potency did not decay, as it did in the leaves; and second, it could be transported in a fraction of the volume required to ship coca leaf. The young William Halsted, later to become the father of American surgery, showed that injecting cocaine close to a nerve paralysed its action, and thus opened up a great range of operations which could be performed under a nerve block, without a hazardous general anaesthetic.

Towards the end of the nineteenth century the more responsible doctors were becoming aware that cocaine was addictive. A number of household patent medicines contained cocaine, of which 'Ryno's Hay Fever and Catarrh Remedy' was the most famous. It also came in many guises – toothpaste, cigarettes, coca tea and chocolates, and it 'cured' depression, nervous exhaustion and toothache. More and more complications and side-effects, and even deaths, were being recorded, as well as abundant evidence of its addictive potential. A second wave of complications was observed around 1910 in those who were using cocaine for hedonistic, rather than medicinal, purposes.

In the early twentieth century cocaine acquired a dark reputation. It was by then being used for purely pleasurable purposes. It became associated with the bohemians of the Decadent Movement, and low-life both in America and Europe. It was the black stevedores of the American South who discovered that it could be snorted up the nose – much cheaper than buying a syringe to inject it. From 1912 onwards, the history of cocaine becomes one of largely ineffective attempts to control its availability, and to eliminate its use. The International Opium Convention at The Hague of 1912 started it all off. Various international laws and conventions under the auspices of the League of Nations, and later the United Nations, required increasingly suppressive action.

None of this, however, curbed the appetite or demand for cocaine, or other drugs. The suspicion that London prostitutes were selling cocaine to troops on leave resulted in the Defence of the Realm Act Regulation 40B, in July 1916. The particularly relaxed attitude to drugs in Japan enabled the large and peculiarly Japanese commercial concerns, which were a combination of large companies, the government and the Imperial family, to produce and trade in cocaine all over the Orient, often transported by the Japanese army and navy. The market for legitimate cocaine had almost disappeared by the 1920s, but the European and American drug companies were still producing great quantities of cocaine. They were well aware that much of their output was being diverted to the black market. Indeed, European producers had been exporting large quantities of narcotics to the Far East since the turn of the century.

The Japanese continued to refine the potent Javanese coca leaves, which they had also planted in Taiwan, Okinawa and Iwo Jima, and by the early 1930s they had become the world's biggest suppliers of cocaine, most of it to the burgeoning black market in China and elsewhere in the Far East. The main purpose of this illegal trade was to make enough money to fund their imperial adventures in Manchuria and Northern China. It later became evident that Japan had been keeping two sets of books to avoid trouble with the League of Nations. But these activities came to an end with the outbreak of the Second World War.

In 1979, the Marxist Sandinista movement took power in Nicaragua. They had been formed in 1961 in response to the corruption and brutality of President Samoza. Once in power, they joined with President Castro of Cuba in supporting other communist movements in the area. Once President Reagan took office in 1981, he committed the CIA to covert anti-Sandinista operations. This involved training and arming the 'Contras' – an anti-communist militia based on the remnants of President Samoza's National Guard. It was quickly evident that the Contras were heavily involved in smuggling cocaine from Colombia into America. This proved too much for Congress, which cut off aid to the Contras in 1984, presenting a problem to President Reagan. Colonel Oliver North provided the solution. He was working in the office of the National Security Advisor and devised a scheme for continuing to fund the Contras, which became known as the 'Iran-Contra Affair'. US arms were being sold to Iran, and the payments were to be used to buy arms for the Contras.

American appetites for cocaine started to rise during the 1960s, but came under the Controlled Substances Act only in

1970. Its popularity grew fast nevertheless, as did the supply, mainly smuggled in from Colombia through the Caribbean. In the early 1980s, this led to a glut in the cities and falling prices, resulting in the surplus being converted into 'crack' – a form of cocaine which is smoked, reaching the brain in seconds and producing a very intense high.

By 1986, one in eleven of the US population admitted to having use cocaine at some time. Crime soared, gangs of suppliers fought each other on the streets, the number of users rose, and the purity of street drugs rose while their price fell. And there were allegations that much of this activity was run by the Nicaraguans expressly to finance the Contra war.

Meanwhile, the CIA, because of their need to arm and supply the Contras, found themselves doing deals with known cocaine smugglers. Planes flying arms southwards were using small clandestine airstrips in Honduras or Costa Rica, which also belonged to those who were flying cocaine into America. Indeed, some of the CIA aircraft themselves flew drugs north, rather than return empty. It was a cynical and murky business, but apparently justified in the name of fighting communism. And for a time in the late 1980s, those involved were shielded from investigation by the US authorities.

In 1986, the Bolivian government, supported by US troops, moved against traffickers and cocaine production facilities, capturing 27 tonnes of cocaine. It was largely a cosmetic exercise since 70 per cent of the Bolivian GDP was related to cocaine, and the effect on supplies in the US was only temporary. Nevertheless it marked the start of increasingly interventionist policy moves by the US in South America. In 1989, the US invaded Panama and arrested dictator General Noriega, a past CIA paid agent, and a major cocaine smuggler.

In Colombia, the threat of extradition to America prompted the enormously rich and powerful cartels into action. A shockingly vicious and ruthless campaign of murder and bombing mounted by the Medellin cartel, culminated in the blowing up of an airliner flying from Bogotá to Medellin. But there were a number of notable successes in the fight against the drug barons. Many were captured and tried, or extradited to the US, and some were killed. Pablo Escobar, the biggest godfather in the Medellin cartel, surrendered to the authorities on condition that he was not extradited, but he escaped and was then killed in a shoot-out.

President Bush Sr decided that effective control of the cocaine trade depended upon action by and with the main producers. He devised the 'Andean strategy', a programme of military support, help with law enforcement, and economic aid to Colombia, Bolivia and Peru. In February 1990 he travelled to Cartegena in Colombia to sign an agreement binding the US to do all in its power to reduce demand for drugs at home, and the Andean countries to attack production and trafficking by all possible means. Andean countries also impressed upon the President the importance of creating new trade opportunities which would provide alternative work for the cocaine producers.

The cartels responded by changing their trafficking routes and methods. Poorer countries, like Nicaragua, with high unemployment, were happy to play their part. In 1994, cocaine, heroin and marijuana were once again pouring into the US through borders as leaky as a colander, assisted, it is said, by the terms of the 1992 North American Free Trade Agreement. There was virtually limitless money at the disposal of the smugglers, for their profits were vast, and they used it to buy planes and fast boats, which were a match for anything the Americans were using. By the time of the 1992 Presidential election, it was clear that interdiction had failed. President Clinton, newly appointed, promised to put more effort into treatment and addiction prevention. But he was under constant pressure from the drug warriors in Congress, and he continued to pursue hard-line policies.

By 1996, not much had changed, and the Organization of American States agreed a hemispheric anti-drug programme. It required an improbable degree of commitment from numerous countries. And the rest of the world was beginning to weary of US pressure to comply with its policies, which everyone but the US government could see was achieving very little. But this did not dampen American enthusiasm for even heavier commitment in South America.

'Plan Colombia' was an ambitious proposal by President Andrés Pastrana, aimed at solving many of Colombia's economic and political problems. It was to cost $7.5 billion over two years. Money was to come from the United States, the European Union, the World Bank, and other major lenders. Washington provided $1.3 billion, military helicopters, and trainers for local forces. Seen by the Colombian President as a way of ending the civil war between Marxist guerrilla insurgents and right-wing paramilitaries, all of whom trafficked in drugs or kidnapped wealthy Colombians to pay for their activities, Pastrana proved adept at squeezing more and more aid out of America, proving to be an attraction to other South American countries to join the Plan which they had earlier resisted.

President Bush Jr inherited the policy from President Clinton, and pursued it enthusiastically. But civil wars are rarely settled by fighting, and negotiations broke down. Much of the aid went to the military or the police, who were responsible for massive human rights abuses, which worried Congress. The shortfall in Colombian cocaine was simply made up from elsewhere. America was getting very poor value for its money, but the general provisions of Plan Colombia continue to this day.

American drug policy in South America has three elements: what it calls 'interdiction' or disruption of drug trafficking routes; narcotic crop eradication; and crop substitution through alternative development programmes. All three are flawed policies. In reality, little more than 10 per cent of the drugs entering the US are intercepted. Forced spraying of coca bushes with weed killer from the air almost always kills other food crops as well, thus increasing rural poverty, and hence support for left-wing insurgent movements. Compensated eradication often proved to be a way of taking American money, and using it to plant new coca bushes in more remote locations. And the concentration on cocaine eradication draws attention and resources away from tackling the flourishing heroin trade. Furthermore, reduction of the coca crop puts prices up, and hence provides more incentive for clandestine planting. Coca crop substitutes have been a complete failure, for coca growing is ten to fifty times more lucrative than any other agricultural crop. It will grow in poor soil on steep slopes, start producing in eighteen months, yield up to six crops of leaves a year, has a life of twenty-five years, and incurs no transport costs since buyers will go to the farmers and take the leaves away. Furthermore, because the crop is illegal, growers do not have to engage with any government bureaucracy at all.

Money to be made by drug trafficking is so huge that corruption is inevitable and endemic, and with it comes violence on a major scale. Corruption and violence are eating away the rule of law, and the governability of these countries. American policies require the Andean countries to give up a highly significant proportion of their Gross Domestic Product, which, being illegal, is difficult to determine exactly how much that is. And all these efforts and sacrifices made no difference to the price of cocaine in America's cities.

Mexican drug cartels owe their origin to a former Federal police agent, Felix Gallardo. During the 1980s he controlled the illegal drug trade in Mexico, and the smuggling routes into the US. Organized crime had long existed, which trafficked illegal immigrants, liquor and other contraband, across the border into America. Gallardo smuggled Mexican marijuana and heroin into the US, and he soon linked up with the Medellin cartel, then run by Pablo Escobar. Aware of the constant risk of arrest, he decided to break up his then monopoly, and so the cartels were born.

Following the death of Pablo Escobar in 1993, and some successes by the Colombian authorities, the notorious Colombian cartels went into decline. At about the same time, increased vigilance by the US authorities in southern Florida and the Caribbean forced a change in the smuggling routes. Cocaine started to flow north from Colombia through Central America into Mexico, where the cartels were well organized, and they took over seamlessly the fantastically profitable business of trafficking cocaine as well. Today they control about 70 per cent of the foreign narcotics trade in the US. In addition to cocaine, they smuggle marijuana, heroin and methylamphetamines, and on the return journey they bring back large amounts of cash, following the increasingly effective measures to stop money laundering. They also smuggle guns from the US and elsewhere, and deal in arms stolen from the police or the armed forces.

Cartels have remained wholesalers, leaving the retail distribution of drugs to local criminal gangs. In recent years they have extended their criminal activities to major cities in the USA. They also control large areas of a number of Mexican states, numbers of cities, and they are now getting involved in electoral politics. Their vast incomes, estimated to be several tens of billions of dollars a year, enable them to buy the protection of politicians, and to corrupt senior police and military officers. The sickening and murderous violence which goes with all this is discussed elsewhere in this book.

In 2000, Vicente Fox was elected President of Mexico. For the previous seventy-two years the country had been ruled by the Institutional Revolutionary Party (PRI). It had descended into a distinctly un-revolutionary morass of corrupt patronage, in which almost every facet of life was controlled by party politics. President Fox was the leader and co-founder of the National Action Party (PAN). He espoused a free-market capitalist meritocracy. The cartels had been able to thrive in the paternalistic *laissez faire* atmosphere of the PRI, but a new wind was now blowing through politics, and the cartels had to look very hard at what they were doing, and how they did it. Cocaine consumption was declining in the US so they returned to trafficking heroin, and added the manufactured drug, methylamphetamine, to their product range.

Amid increasing violence from the cartels as they sought to dominate each other and the crossing points on the border,

President Fox sent small numbers of troops to the border to fight the cartels, with little apparent success. In principle he supported the American prohibitionist stance while he was in power, but in 2010 he came out strongly in favour of legalizing drugs as being the only way to curb the power and influence of the cartels. These views were not shared by his successor, President Felipe Calderón, who was elected in 2006. He soon sent 6,500 federal troops to the border to end the drug violence there. This marked the start of the Mexican drug war, which now involves about 45,000 troops, as well as state and federal police forces. Meanwhile, the murderous mayhem continues, and the corruption unleashed by the narco-billions makes it almost impossible to know which senior officials, police or military officers are loyal, and which are in the pay of the cartels. The traffickers are becoming more sophisticated by the year. Drugs are now being smuggled in home-made submarines, which are difficult to find and capture.

The intensification of this war brings its difficulties when the military increasingly have to operate as untrained civilian police. Increasing numbers of human rights violations are being reported – a situation being made worse by the corruption of politicians and the judiciary.

In 2008, the Mérida Initiative was signed by President Bush Jr. Its aim was to provide further support to Mexico, Central America, the Dominican Republic and Haiti, in the fight against the cartels and cross-border trafficking. It was to provide equipment, military hardware, training, expertise and money to bolster the fight on all fronts by increasing the effectiveness of their institutions.

There have been significant successes. The power of the cartels is declining, there have been many drug seizures, and many arrests of cartel members. Criminals have been extradited to America and tried. But large numbers of people have died, and the most sickening violence remains common in many parts of the country. It has yet to be seen if the innocent population of Mexico will continue to tolerate the enormous expense and disruption which the war continues to bring.

In 1994, the Rand Corporation published a study on the US efforts to stop the cocaine trade.[84] It found that every dollar spent on eradicating coca plants in South America returned 17 cents, efforts to prevent trafficking between South and North America returned 32 cents, domestic law enforcement by the police and customs services returned 52 cents, and every dollar spent on the treatment of users yielded $7.48. These are impressive figures, but there is not a lot of evidence that anybody has taken much notice of them.

Heroin, and the countries where it is grown

The opium poppy, *Papaver somniferum*, is an undemanding plant. It will grow in almost any temperate climate, and seeds itself readily. This is reflected in the fact that, historically, it has been grown in many parts of the world, but today 90 per cent of the world's raw opium, from which heroin is produced, comes from Afghanistan. When the flower is over and the petals fall, an inverted conical seed-head with a frill on its top is left. When scored with a knife before it desiccates, a resinous sap oozes out which can be collected for the next few days. The sticky exudate is then dried. It is known as raw opium.

Evidence suggests that the opium poppy became domesticated in the western Mediterranean area sometime between 7000 and 5000 BC. We know that it played an important role in ancient Egypt, and it was probably used by priests on important religious occasions. It was imported originally from Cyprus in small clay pots which look strikingly like an inverted poppy seed-head. These have been found in Egypt, from which traces of opium have recently been identified by mass-spectroscopy. Most were found at Tel-el-Amarna, the city of Akhenaton. There is evidence of the use of opium in Crete in the late Minoan III period, during religious ceremonies, to induce the necessary state of mind to perform sacred rites. We also know that the poppy became widely distributed in the then known world, which suggests strongly that its medicinal and narcotic properties were known. Seeds have been found in many Neolithic sites in Switzerland, Germany, Italy, England and Poland. Poppy seeds were used in baking and to extract a culinary oil, but it is unlikely that these were their sole uses.

From the Ancient Egyptians onwards, every civilization knew and used opium. The Sumerians, the Babylonians and the Assyrians all wrote about its properties, and how to harvest it. The Greeks were well aware of its therapeutic properties, though there is no real evidence that they used it as an intoxicant. It is mentioned in the botanical works of Theophrastus in 360 BC, and described in the writings of the military physician, Discorides, two hundred years later. It also plays a part in the Greek myths. The Romans acquired their knowledge of opium from the Greeks. It was extensively used by Galen, the founder of scientific medicine, who may have been responsible for formulating mithridate, a mixture of opium and honey or jam to make the bitterness of opium more palatable. It was also well known to Avicenna (Ibn-Sina), the great eleventh-century Persian physician and sage.

It was the Arabs, as the great traders of the time, who spread the cultivation and use of opium to Persia, to India, and ultimately to China, where it first appears in the medical texts in the eighth century AD. Seven hundred years later there is evidence that opium started to be used for hedonistic purposes on a large scale in Persia and parts of India. It was grown throughout the Mughal Empire, and it provided significant revenue for the great Emperor Akhbar. By this time there were two main areas in India which grew opium – Bengal opium on the banks of the River Ganges inland from Calcutta, and Malwa opium, inland from Bombay on the west coast.

The Portuguese were the first to recognize the potential of the opium trade. They started to export Malwa opium to China, but they had to compete aggressively with Indian and Arab merchants. They also exported Brazilian tobacco, which the Chinese were soon growing themselves. But it was the pipe, introduced by the Spanish, charged with tobacco and opium, which ensured the success of the opium trade, because it became the usual way to smoke opium in China. In the early seventeenth century the Dutch started exporting Bengal opium to their trading posts in Java. It proved to be a spectacularly profitable trade for the Dutch East India Company.

The British were slow to exploit the opium trade. It was not until 1757 that the British took Bengal by force of arms, and with it the opium trade based on Patna. The East India Company established a monopoly over the growing and sale of Bengal opium, which they sold at their Calcutta auctions to European merchants who shipped it to China. In this way the East India Company itself was not directly flouting the 1729 ban by the Emperor of China on smoking opium. The opium trade was pursued energetically by the Company until it lost its charter in 1834. Britain had developed a great appetite for tea, silk and porcelain, but there was no demand in China for British goods. The tax levied in Britain on Chinese tea paid half the total cost of the Royal Navy. Consequently these imports had to be paid for in silver, and by 1800 China possessed half the silver in the world. Exporting opium to China was the obvious answer, both for India and Britain.

After the charter ended in 1834, the trade was opened up to private interests, of which the best known was Jardine Matheson. The competition was fierce, particularly between the British and the Americans. Fast and well-armed ships were designed which could do three round trips from India to China in the year. They traded with the only 'open' port in China – Canton, but in order to circumvent the Emperor's ban on the importation of opium, the traders unloaded their cargoes at Lintin island, which lay between Macao and Hong Kong, whence they were spirited away by Chinese 'chop boats'. They then proceeded, empty, up to the European warehouses in Canton to load their tea and other cargoes.

In 1839, in the face of mounting corruption, the Chinese appointed a new governor of Canton to put an end to the opium trade. It led to the First Opium War, which ended in 1842 with the Treaty of Nanking. This required the Chinese to pay heavy indemnities, ceding Hong Kong to Britain, and nominating other ports where Europeans could trade. But in spite of overwhelming successes for British arms, the Emperor could not be made to budge on his absolute refusal to contemplate legalizing the opium trade. This was a blow to Palmerston's determination to increase trade with China to make up for the loss of markets in Europe and America.

For the next fifteen years or so, the illicit trade in opium continued, based in Hong Kong. Large numbers of Chinese coolies left to work in the new gold mines and railway building in California, and they took their opium with them. In mainland China, corruption grew, and the Taiping movement developed in opposition to the debauched Emperor and his opium-smoking wife.

Britain was still itching to open up trade with China, and to enforce the terms of the Treaty of Nanking. A trivial incident sparked off the Second Opium War in 1856. Initially the fanatical and tyrannical Viceroy Ye Mingchen had a number of successes, including burning down the European factories, and driving British and American shipping out of the Pearl River. There was mass emigration by the more prosperous Hong Kong Chinese to California and Australia. Slowly a military force of British, French, American and Russians gathered and attacked Canton. In the face of overwhelming force of arms the Chinese signed the Treaty of Tientsin. This gave more access to Chinese markets, and finally agreed the legalization of opium.

There was soon to be more trouble in Canton, and in Peking the authorities had come to believe that, backed by the Mongolian Prince Seng and his cavalry, Chinese arms could succeed against the Europeans. Initially they put up stiff resistance, but were ultimately no match for the new 25-pounder Armstrong field gun. After Peking rejected an ultimatum, a major force of British, French and Indian troops advanced on, and eventually entered, Peking. Doubtless with the uncompromising words of Palmerston ringing in his ears, the British commander, Lord Elgin, decided to complete the destruction of the imperial Summer Palace, an act of unforgivable vandalism and plunder, which horrified the French commander, Baron Gross.

The Opium Wars were imperial adventures by British arms, supremely confident following the Napoleonic wars, with the intention of opening up new markets for British goods. They were a lasting humiliation for the Chinese, which the return of Hong Kong in 1997 may have gone some way to assuage.

As a post-script to this story, the total exports of opium from India, mostly going to China, rose from 58,681 chests a year in 1859-60 to 105,508 twenty years later. By that time China was growing great quantities itself, and by 1900 there were 13.5 million addicts in the country. The opium trade was finally stopped in 1907. But opium continued to be used by huge numbers of Chinese until the practice was ruthlessly suppressed by the new communist government in 1947.

Southeast Asia remained a minor producer of opium until the 1950s, in spite of the consumption of a great deal in the opium dens of Bangkok and Saigon, and elsewhere. This situation was to change drastically. By the 1980s the 'Golden triangle' – the highland areas of Burma, Thailand and Laos – was to become the largest producer in the world, with an output of over 3,300 tonnes of raw opium annually. For many years the production had been held down by the British and French colonial powers, and by the kingdom of Siam, whose monopolies taxed and controlled the importation of opium, and suppressed local production. After the communists took over in China in 1947, and outlawed opium growing, much of the crop grown in Yunnan and Szechwan was smuggled across the border into the Shan States of Burma, where it undercut the local monopoly prices.

But by 1955 external sources of opium had all but dried up, leaving thousands of addicts with no supply. This was the result of successful suppression of poppy growing in western China, international agreement in 1953 to stop exportation of opium, and the abolition of opium growing in Iran in 1955, which had previously been a major supplier to Southeast Asia.

Bereft of opium, these wretched addicts would have been forced to give it up if the drought had lasted. But these events had the predictable result of stimulating production in Afghanistan and Turkey, and some new players entered the game. The great Satan of communism was to lead America and its allies into two major and prolonged wars in Korea and Vietnam, but the French and the CIA were also engaged in covert anti-communist warfare in Southeast Asia. Both, for different reasons, funded their activities by clandestine involvement in the opium trade.

The French, who had been in Indochina since the 1880s, were starved of funds to fight a seemingly inconclusive and unpopular war against communist guerrillas. Paris saw the reconstruction of war-torn France and its institutions as a more important use of money. Opium was growing in Laos, and the opium dens of Saigon had none, so putting them together at a huge profit was the obvious solution. The CIA, on the other hand, was well-funded. Local alliances with power brokers or warlords made the money go much further, but it also inevitably led to involvement in the opium trade, which in turn funded more activity.

In May 1954, French power in the region came to an end at Dien Bien Phu. The CIA took over when the French departed. There was little or no involvement of US combat troops. The war against communism was fought by proxy armies armed, trained and equipped by the CIA. Loyalty was bought with dollars and military hardware. The main client forces were the remnants of Chiang Kai-shek's Nationalist army, which had fled into the Shan States in northern Burma; the Hmong hill tribes, who fielded an army of 30,000 tough and tenacious fighters, which would accept huge losses; and The Royal Laotian army and air-force. All of these forces were deeply involved in growing and trafficking opium, and in some cases, converting it into heroin. It would have been impossible to do business with any of these groups without becoming complicit in the opium trade.

Once the political decision to combat communism by all means available had been taken, full involvement was inevitable.

It also meant getting into bed with some very unsavoury and ruthless crooks, who used their positions to enrich themselves on an enormous scale. General Phao, the commander of the Thai police, was the CIA's chief client in Thailand. Supplies of opium were transported, in some cases in unmarked C-47 transport planes, to Bangkok and delivered to General Phao, who distributed it for local consumption, and for export, at great profit to himself. General Ouane Rattikone was commander of the Laotian army, and an ambitious drug baron, who was determined to control the flow of opium from Burma to the laboratories on the Thai-Burma-Laotian border, some of which he owned.

It was one of his laboratories, just inside Laos, which produced the purest 'number 4 heroin' which was sold, with enormous profit, by the Vietnamese to the GIs fighting the Korean war. At one point there were an estimated 30,000 serving American troops using it. This in turn was one of the reasons that President Nixon in 1971 declared his 'War on Drugs'. Another major figure was Khun Sa, a young Shan warlord who supplied General Rattikone with opium. After a long career of varying fortunes, he came to control 80 per cent of Burma's opium production and half the world's supply of heroin. In 1996 he eventually surrendered to the Burmese army in a nauseatingly theatrical ceremony in front of television cameras, and was welcomed by the Rangoon government.

The price of the continuing loyalty of the Hmong was acceptance of their involvement in the opium trade, and the transportation of the raw opium to local markets from their laboratories, one of which was situated at the CIA's Laotian headquarters at Long Tieng, and run by people on the CIA's payroll. The distribution of the opium, morphine base and heroin required aircraft, and the few remaining French and Corsican gangsters in the region started small charter airlines, collectively known as Air Opium. They were later superseded by the planes and helicopters of Air America, the CIA's own charter airline.

Two years of drought in the Golden Triangle in the early 1970s, and another failure of the monsoon rains in 1979, were the catalysts for major increases in exports of heroin from Central Asia to the West. This was grown in Pakistan and Afghanistan, and converted into heroin in laboratories just inside Pakistan. Intense American pressure on Pakistan drove down their opium growing, but the gap in production was immediately made good from Afghanistan.

In 1979, the Russians invaded Afghanistan, and once again prompted a major CIA operation. A year before, communist army officers had overthrown the Afghan dictator. President Carter acted swiftly by arming the Afghan resistance, and stirring up Islamic fundamentalism in Soviet Central Asia, with the intention of making difficulties for the Russians. Little did he realize how important that decision would become. The CIA chose to channel its support to the mujahedin through the Pakistani military intelligence organization, the ISI. Astonishingly the CIA took this organization's advice to support its client, Gulbuddin Hekmatyar, who proved to be incompetent, savage, a fundamentalist, and a controlling figure in the drug trade. Raw opium started to flood out of Afghanistan into the lawless tribal areas of northern Pakistan, where it was refined into heroin. Much of it was shipped out in military trucks which had delivered supplies to the CIA.

Early in 1989, the Soviet army withdrew from Afghanistan, leaving a country awash with guns and military equipment, which the strongest used to enforce their power over their rivals. Opium was the only source of money in a ravaged and deserted country, and the means of processing it and getting to the lucrative markets of the West were in place, thanks to the CIA.

The end of communism and the independence of the ex-Soviet Central Asian republics saw a contagious outbreak of ethnic insurgency stretching from Uzbekistan to Bosnia, much of it paid for by heroin. The Afghan crop grew relentlessly, and the warlords were left to slug it out in a bitter and savage civil war. When their client, Hekmatyar, failed to form a government, the ISI backed the formation of a new Pashtun force, the Taliban. Once in power, the Taliban set about collecting large tax revenues of opium in kind, which they sold to heroin laboratories. They presided over a state totally dependent on opium growing and refining, and their ban on educating women unwittingly produced a huge low-cost labour force to sustain and increase opium production, which is very labour intensive.

After two years of disastrous drought forced his hand, the Taliban leader, Mullah Omar, offered a cessation of all opium cultivation in exchange for international recognition. The ban came into force in July 2000. They were, nevertheless, able to profit by the sharp rise in the price of drugs that the ban produced, by selling their hoarded stocks. However, the United Nations were able to confirm that opium production had declined by 94 per cent. It was an extraordinary act of national suicide, bringing poverty and destitution to much of the population. The regime collapsed in October 2001. Within days the Taliban rescinded their prohibition on opium growing. In no time gardens and fields were a riot of red and white and pink poppies. A new crop of warlords came out of hiding, and the CIA bribed the Pashtun leaders to drive out the remaining Taliban, but, of course, they were all also drug traffickers, and their loyalty went to the highest bidder.

Mohammed Karzai, the new prime minister, offered opium eradication in exchange for help with crop substitution, reconstruction, and technical support of many kinds. After the initial fanfare of enthusiasm died down, the international community promised just $4 billion of the necessary $10 billion for national reconstruction, and only 5 per cent of the food aid immediately required. Crop eradication payments were woefully inadequate. Heroin remained the only source of money, and became the local currency. Meanwhile the size of the crop grew year upon year.

In 2007 opium production in Afghanistan reached 8,890 tonnes, a rise of 34 per cent from the record levels of 2006. This represented 93 per cent of the world's supply, and far outstripped global demand, estimated at 4,500 tonnes.[82] Overproduction continued in 2008 and 2009. Britain and other countries are formally committed to the destruction of the poppy crop in Afghanistan, but in practice little is done. There are no substitute crops that can bring the farmers anything like the return that poppies do. If it were possible to eradicate poppy growing it would be the most effective recruiting sergeant the Taliban could wish for.

For the past thirty years the international community has spent huge sums of money on this problem, though never enough to make a real difference. Interdiction, crop eradication, crop substitution and 'alternative livelihoods' have all been tried, with little lasting success. In any country over which central government does not have firm and effective control, production limitation is a mirage. Even the recurrent suggestion that the West should buy up the opium crop and turn it into pharmacological heroin or morphine, of which there is said to be a shortage, is fraught with difficulties. In reality there is no worldwide shortage of opiate drugs for medicinal use – it is simply that they are not released for use because they are wrongly assumed by the authorities in many countries to lead to addiction.

But the bull-headed policies of the past few years are giving way to more considered and effective strategies. Lessons are being learned. Crop eradication simply increases poverty and hands political capital to the warlords or the Taliban, who seek to protect the farmers against crop destruction and become legitimized in the eyes of the local population. This, in turn, ensures that the intelligence, so vital to the government's fight against insurgencies, dries up.

Where payment for crop destruction has been tried, the money invariably ends up in the wrong hands, and further antagonizes the wretched farmers. Current policy is directed towards increasing government control over rural areas, and eradication, accompanied by practical and realistic schemes to provide alternative livelihoods. We are left with the irony that the Taliban was easily able to stop opium farming, while nearly ten years of 'democratic' government has seen record crops. It is a complex problem, but it may well be true that opium production is more a consequence of Afghanistan's lawlessness, instability and poverty, than its cause.

The Effects on Transit States

As we have noted, the value of the North American cocaine market has fallen dramatically in the past ten years, but has been more than made up by a big increase in European consumption – accompanied by new patterns of trafficking. In the 1970s and 1980s, most cocaine bound for the US was shipped through the Caribbean and Florida. Successful measures to stop the smugglers, involving increasingly high-tech equipment, gradually forced them to alter their tactics. More and more cocaine began reaching the US across the Mexican border, which came to be controlled by the Mexican cartels, who had wrested the trade from their Colombian suppliers. Other Caribbean countries that had been involved in the trade were Jamaica, The Dominican Republic, Trinidad and Tobago, and the Dutch Antilles, which shipped cocaine from Venezuela by air to Holland.

Displaced by the Central American countries of Guatemala, El Salvador, Honduras and Belize as trafficking through the Caribbean declined, both Guatemala and El Salvador have been involved in prolonged and brutal civil wars. Both countries are notable for extreme inequalities in income distribution and not surprisingly, they are areas of political instability, militias and uncertain justice.

All the countries through which cocaine is smuggled have grotesquely high murder rates – among the highest in the world. They are led by Honduras, in which there are nearly twelve times more violent deaths than in the US, and thirty-six times more than in Canada.[83] Victims are all involved in drug smuggling.

Their people though, are well-organized and sophisticated. In many cases they have corrupted very senior police officers and the heads of drug enforcement agencies. They commit many high profile murders of officials who dare to oppose them. The stain of corruption spreads far and wide to criminal justice officials, legislators, and members of local and state government.

Much the same thing has been happening in West Africa. This region contains some of the poorest and least developed nations in the world. Nine such countries were on a global list of the twenty-five with the highest risks of instability: Niger, Mali, Sierra Leone, Liberia, Mauritania, Guinea-Bissau, Guinea, Côte d'Ivoire and Benin. Since 2004 there has been evidence of large-scale trafficking in cocaine through West Africa, organized largely by the Mexican cartels. This followed the shift in the global market away from North America to Europe. Two centres developed, one in the north, based on Guinea and Guinea-Bissau, and the other in the Bight of Benin. Both seem to have been run by Nigerians. Ships arriving from South America were unloaded onto small coastal craft, their cargoes repackaged and re-directed to European buyers. Meanwhile, the West Africans were paid in kind, and allowed to keep a third of the shipments for their own purposes. Most of this was then smuggled into Europe by commercial air couriers – 'drug mules'.

In 2008, things started to change. International efforts to stop this trade began to bear fruit, and there were a number of high level murders and defections in Guinea and Guinea-Bissau.[84] These were the inevitable consequences of the very high value of cocaine compared to local GDPs. For example, the GDP of Guinea-Bissau in 2008 was $400 million. Very quickly senior military figures took over the drug trade, and issued death threats to anyone who looked as if they might challenge them.

Murders and attempted coups plunged the country into ungovernable chaos. Similar events unfolded in Guinea, and there is evidence that control of the northern hub then moved to the Gambia. Very recently the disputed election result in Côte d'Ivoire has brought that country to the brink of civil war. And there is now evidence of the shadowy presence in West Africa of associates of Al Qaeda, who are certainly well paid for providing 'services' to the smugglers.

Similar events unfold wherever the flood of drug money touches poor countries. There is no chance of preventing this, or of returning these nations to honest government. The only possible remedy is to remove the money, and the only way to do this is to legalize the drug trade, and so make cocaine a commodity like coffee and many others, to be traded at a price determined by a legal and free market.

7　The Case for Legalization

Whenever the subject of drugs is raised it is likely to provoke an argument. It is an issue about which most people have strong views. It must be said, however, that the strength of their feelings is often in inverse ratio to the depth of knowledge informing their beliefs. Few are sufficiently indifferent not to enter the debate. Opinions grow increasingly polarized and entrenched: on the one hand most favour prohibition, though usually choose to ignore the current ubiquity of drugs; on the other hand, a growing minority advocate legalization, though usually without any understanding of its rational basis. Ignorance on this subject, as on many others, is vocal. Both viewpoints are exercised by commentators in the press, who write as if it was so obvious that their particular arguments will crack the problems, that there can be no further discussion. But we must accept that nothing will ever do that – whatever accommodation society eventually reaches with the existence of drugs will simply be the least bad option.

There is nothing good about illegal drugs. But they are here and the appetite for them is inextinguishable. No rational person can believe that they can be made to go away. We must work within these realities. Unfettered availability has developed in the face of prohibition, indeed, as a consequence of uncontrolled markets run by criminals.

A legalization policy has at its centre the determination to abolish the criminal market, and put in its place a market that is both regulated and controlled. Drug legalization is the necessary prerequisite, since it is not possible to have a legal market in illegal goods.

Legalization is neither philosophical or libertarian. Nor, most emphatically, should it be thought of as a silver bullet that would prove to be 'the answer' to the problem of drug use. It should be seen as one step, albeit a very important one, towards addressing and ameliorating the harm which drugs bring to all societies. Legalization would lead to a tightly controlled system for the sale of mind-altering substances in order to contain the consequences of their use or abuse, reduce harm, assure and control strengths and purities, guarantee sterility where appropriate, and secure proper labelling. Furthermore, market forces would determine prices, and taxes could be raised on every purchase. We have many years experience of running parallel markets. Legalization is often misrepresented as a policy to 'liberalize' or 'relax' drug laws. This is the opposite of the truth.

The libertarian principle enjoys much support. It states that citizens should be allowed to do what they want, so long as they are adults, know the risks, do no harm to others and impose no costs on the public purse. John Stuart Mill believed that the state had no right to intervene, even to prevent individuals from harming themselves. Freedom of personal choice is an important and basic principle, and it is difficult to see why, for example, the occasional use of cannabis or a tablet of ecstasy should be prohibited by the majesty of the law, when smoking and drinking go uncensored.

Mark Thornton and Milton Friedman, free marketeers both, argue that market forces are superior to those imposed by governments. Thomas Szasz believes that drug control is an illegal act, the consequences of which are of no account, because only the merits or defects of the argument concern him.[85] Douglas Husak takes a different position.[86] He wishes to determine whether there are principled reasons for denying that adults should be permitted to use recreational drugs. He questions whether the state has the right to punish adult users of some drugs but not of others. His arguments are impeccable, and he concludes that there are currently no just and acceptable reasons for criminalizing the use of any recreational drugs. His underlying concern is the relationship between citizens and the state, and the balance between the state power and the rights of its citizens. These are arresting and important issues which provide a sound theoretical basis for the policy of legalization, but they leave untouched many of the more practical and thorny problems which legalizers must address before formulating and implementing pragmatic policy decisions.

Some prohibitionists at least have a philosophical basis to support their beliefs. Some hold that it is morally wrong to take any psychoactive or intoxicating drug, other than for a strictly necessary medical indication. For those who hold this view, prohibition is the only choice.

Morality is about right and wrong, or good and evil. But here we have a difficulty. The concept of good and evil is drawn from the values of systems of belief. In today's secular society this means less than it used to. Even right and wrong present problems, for who is to be the arbiter? The individual citizen? A wise man who is paid to decide? The majority view? The government? And views change, sometimes quite quickly. It is a fair bet that most people today would not regard it as morally wrong to take a psychoactive drug, and if alcohol were included, there would be no contest. Most people, therefore, do not take the prohibitionist view on such uncompromising grounds. But it is still an honest and intellectually respectable stance, though whether it has the power or a mandate to out-rank all other arguments, is much more doubtful. It is sometimes called the evangelical prohibitionist stance.

But moral purity has a price and the holders of such views must take their share of responsibility for the consequences of prohibition. As we have seen, murder, violence, corruption, property crime and the criminalization and imprisonment of hundreds of thousands of their fellow citizens, are all a direct result of the illegality of drugs, not of drugs themselves. That is a heavy burden to bear.

Those prohibitionists who do not take such a high-minded stance on drug use must depend on a much less convincing rationale to legitimize their views. It is to be found in a book entitled *Body Count*, two of the three authors of which were former US Drug Tsars.[87] The purpose of the 'War on Drugs', they state, is a moral one, 'to extract a price for transgressing the rights of others'. It is a war against the feral youth of America who indulge in violence and all sorts of crime, consume and deal in drugs, and are responsible for all kinds of communal disorder. Many would say that such deviant behaviour is the consequence of other forces in society, and that the link with drugs is the result of societal breakdown, not its cause.

Prohibition is a radical policy that draws legitimacy from the United Nations Conventions of Illegal Drugs, Psychotropic Drugs, and Drug Trafficking. More importantly, it appears to be an instinctive rather than a reasoned response to the perceived moral threat posed by the 'evil' of drugs, taken primarily to give pleasure. It is as if drugs were some dark force which is said to 'take over' the soul. It is a puritanical point of view, but one which is widely supported. It is also illogical. If pleasure is so objectionable, why does it not include alcohol and tobacco? And what about Viagra? Any discussion about the merits and defects of prohibition should begin with an explanation by those who support the justice of punishing by the law the use of some drugs but not of others.

While prohibition may be said to have the merit of confronting the 'evil' of drugs, it makes no attempt to engage with the very complex and difficult realities of drug taking. On the contrary, it ignores them completely. Nevertheless, prohibition seems to have managed, quite illogically, to have stolen the high ground. It also has another unfortunate effect. It has meant that much of the research in the field of illegal drugs has concentrated on the harm that drugs can cause rather than more constructive studies of how we can mitigate, diminish or eliminate them.

Neither of the policies on offer is entirely right or entirely wrong in every particular. The choice is not as obvious and clear-cut as it is often presented. It is between the discredited and failed policy of prohibition, and the unpredictable consequences of legalization.

Making any far-reaching decision in the presence of uncertainty is unappetizing, and some of the results will not become clear until it is tried. Such a prospect is very unattractive to every political instinct.

If the choices are too difficult, what about maintaining the *status quo*?

This is unsustainable, and will become ever more so. No civilized democracy has ever succeeded in banning something which large numbers of citizens want or like to do, nor will it ever be possible in the future. The spectre of prohibition of alcohol in America (1920-33) ought to have taught us this lesson. Yet the catastrophic 'War on Drugs' in the US, waged at a cost of tens of billions of dollars every year, shows that we learn very slowly, if at all. Drug taking has never been more common, drugs are cheap, and half a million Americans moulder their lives away uselessly and unnecessarily in jail, for non-violent drug offences. There is always a worthwhile price at which criminals will supply prohibited goods. Thus, criminality becomes rampant. There must be a point at which society will no longer tolerate this. At present we struggle, fairly unsuccessfully, to prosecute drug-related criminals, but one day it may seem more logical to eliminate the motives for this criminality.

It is important to make it clear that legalization is not the same thing as decriminalization – another word sometimes used in this context. If, for example, possession of ecstasy were to be decriminalized, it would mean that it would no longer be treated as a crime, though it would remain technically illegal. It would be possible to impose administrative sanctions, such as fines. Legalization means the complete removal of all sanctions on drugs deemed to be for personal use, making possession or use of a drug legal, and not subject to any legal or administrative sanctions. If, however, someone under the influence of a drug was creating a nuisance or caused harm, they would be treated in the same way as similar behaviour caused by the use of alcohol. In all cases, unlicensed dealing in drugs would remain a criminal offence, as it is now.

Drug markets under prohibition are by definition illegal, and hence subject to no regulatory scrutiny or control. The same is the case for drugs bought off the Internet, which are often manufactured in third world countries, and of varied and unpredictable quality. That drugs should be as safe as possible is one of the central principles of the policy of harm reduction. Only if drugs are bought and sold in a legal market is it possible to ensure that what is being sold is of known strength and purity, correctly labelled, and where relevant, guaranteed to be sterile. Strength is currently a particularly important issue with the sale of cannabis, because it can vary greatly.

A legal market would have the crucial advantage that it could be closely regulated. It would be possible to control the manufacture of drugs, and to ensure that they were not sold to under-age users, that there was no advertising, and that drugs were only offered for sale by appropriately licensed outlets.

There are many catastrophes from the use of adulterated or infected drugs: a steady incidence of overdoses, sometimes fatal, from drugs of unknown strength or purity. Illegal markets lead to more extreme and dangerous forms of usage. Purchases have to be completed quickly, because contact with a dealer is dangerous. There is therefore an incentive to use the drugs in such a way as to give the greatest high for your money, which usually means injecting, and using dangerous combinations like 'speedballs' – an injected mixture of heroin and cocaine, often in the form of crack. Such is the urgency to get and maintain the buzz that behaviour becomes more and more risky. We are now seeing the results of this in a rising incidence of HIV/AIDS.

A gentler, more thoughtful use of drugs is thus discouraged in favour of the most addictive and pernicious forms of drug taking. Weaker and less harmful preparations, like poppy-straw tea and opium, have given way to heroin, and chewing coca leaves has been superseded by snorting cocaine and smoking crack. This is a direct consequence of prohibition. The same thing was seen in America during prohibition of alcohol, with the consumption of dangerous and toxic illicit spirits, like 'moonshine' and bathtub gin.

A legal source of drugs would mean that users could obtain their requirements without having to visit dealers, who invariably try to sell them other addictive drugs they had no idea they wanted, or would like. This is a common way in which users come to experiment with other drugs. The sale of Khat, a leaf with mildly stimulatory properties chewed harmlessly by many East Africans, is a good illustration of this point. Because it is legal in Britain, it is sold with fruit and vegetables in Ethiopian and Somali communities, which means that users do not have to go to drug dealers, who might tempt them into other purchases. Furthermore, the price is ten times cheaper than in countries in which Khat is illegal, and sold in criminal markets.

There are three more major arguments in favour of legalization that relate to violence, corruption and crime. They are connected in that they all have to do with money: in the first two cases, the grotesque profits to be made from trafficking drugs; in the other, the consequences of the prices paid on the streets to buy illegal drugs for personal consumption. They play themselves out on very different stages. On the one hand, in the international arena, wherever drugs are being smuggled; and on the other, in much more domestic but ubiquitous settings, anywhere and everywhere where there is a demand for, and hence a market for, drugs.

The international trade in drugs is colossal, particularly for heroin and cocaine. As far as the public is concerned, this is a hidden business, which does not wish to draw attention to itself. It only reaches the public gaze in certain locations like the US-Mexican border. Domestic and small-scale drug dealing can be found in every city, town, and even in many villages, wherever drugs are used, which is almost everywhere in the world.

Thus, all these enormously important problems are caused by money: in the first two cases, far too much of it; and in the third, not enough. It is almost not worthwhile speculating on the profits of the international drug trade – estimates vary widely from $350 billion to twice that amount. An accurate figure will never be known because it is impossible to compute. Obviously it is in the interests of those concerned to say nothing, and to under-estimate if forced into speculating. What is absolutely clear is that it is the most lucrative business in the world, and, as stated several times in this book, it pays no taxes, and is subject to no laws or control. Money is attractive to most people, but to some it is irresistible, and herein lies its power. There are always strings attached to money – very little is given away without an obligation. But the right sum of money can buy almost anything – loyalty, betrayal, violence, murder, insurrection or treason. A few things are not for sale – honesty, integrity, principles and beliefs, but the people who hold to these views are certainly not in the majority.

Money is the midwife of corruption, and the more money available the more corruption there will be. And if we consider First World sums of money on offer in Third World countries where poverty is endemic, unemployment high, social security near non-existent and employment law absent, corruption is inevitable. Add to this inflammatory mix the fact that the already miserable salaries of the police and other government servants are sometimes not paid. The judicial system may be ineffective, making redress for injustices impossible, so many will have to choose between taking dishonest money, or being unable to feed their families. The few highly principled citizens are all the more remarkable, for they place themselves in great danger.

We have seen that drugs are trafficked through some small and sometimes new countries that have autocratic or dishonest governments. They are often unable to control their territory, suffer from insurgencies, and have ineffective legal and government institutions. The dishonest flows of drug money sometimes exceed the GDP of the countries through which they pass. It is obvious what will happen, and it does. Corruption is one of the main causes of state failure, and in many parts of the world, drug money is the commonest cause of corruption.

The border between Mexico and the USA certainly does not fit this description. Mexico is a relatively developed country, rich in human and natural resources, with well-established and reliable institutions. The Mexican government is in control of the country. America is probably still the richest nation in the world with an unprecedentedly powerful military. Yet the border between these two states is over 2,000 miles long, and the strip of land on either side is the scene of a war against the importation of illegal drugs, which is being fought with unimaginable brutality, thanks in considerable part to the virtually uncontrolled availability of American guns. For the Americans, the gun trade is a billion dollar business, and the Mexicans do not have the political will to get serious about it – they have enough to cope with already. It is an irony that the American right, which is so determined to stop people and drugs crossing the border, is equally adamant in opposing controls on the sale of guns to Mexicans or to anyone else.

If guns are the agents of execution, money is the ammunition with which the war is fought. It buys people – both Mexican and American. The situation is so bad that nobody can be trusted, even army generals and police chiefs. They all have their price. It is a nightmare world in which your friend is your enemy. And if you do not want to get involved you have little choice but to look the other way.

Vast quantities of freight are trucked from Mexico to the US, much of it shipped from China through the Mexican Pacific ports. In 2008, goods worth $367 billion crossed the border. In the same year, 41 per cent of this crossed from Nuevo Laredo in Mexico to Laredo in Texas. Ten thousand trucks cross the border here every day – five thousand going north, and five thousand going south, and, in addition, thousands of freight rail wagons.[88] The provisions of the North American Free Trade Agreement (NAFTA) make it virtually impossible to undertake more than the most cursory and random of customs inspections. Best estimates are that 97 per cent of the freight shipped is honest and legitimate. This means that three per cent is contraband, and going into the States, which will be mainly drugs – cocaine, heroin and methylamphetamines. A hundred and fifty trucks of contraband every day at this one crossing. Sixty per cent of the US-Mexican trade crosses at other points – probably another two hundred trucks or more with illegal cargoes. The customs officials and border patrols are either corrupted, or are too intimidated to do their job. They either play the game and get paid, or they refuse to play the game and pay with their lives. Coming back to Mexico, the trucks carry laundered money and guns secreted in their legitimate cargoes.

The border has long been a source of concern to the US, but for a different reason. For nearly a century, itinerant Mexican workers have been crossing illegally into the US in search of work in the industrial and agricultural economies, which need large numbers of low-paid workers. Initially, they entered the US by swimming across the Rio Grande, and hence earned themselves the soubriquet, 'wet backs'. As the border became better patrolled they would cross anywhere they could, even in the Californian desert, where many died lost and waterless. Guiding them across became an industry, and recently it has been taken over by the Mexican cartels as yet another way of making money. Often, once they reach a big American city, they are kidnapped until their relatives can ransom them.

Today the border is marked by more than 600 miles of fence, which is to be extended. It has become a military front line. Where there is no physical barrier there are searchlights, movement sensors and sophisticated listening devices, which alert the heavily armed border patrols. While all this may make it more difficult for illegal immigrants to cross, it will certainly not staunch the haemorrhage of drugs pouring into America.

Recently, there has been a change in the rhetoric. President Obama and Hilary Clinton, his Secretary of State, are now talking about 'co-responsibility' for the border situation, as if to acknowledge that the flow of guns south, and the enormous, though diminished, appetite for cocaine in America is, at least in part, responsible for the prevailing anarchy.

Recent administrations have tried hard to address the situation, with very little success. President Obama has not even been able to extend the ban on the sale of powerful assault weapons enacted by President Clinton, when it expired recently. The constitutional right to bear arms seems to be unassailable, and nobody knows how to curb the appetite for drugs. Good police work based on covert intelligence is obviously desirable, but it will not do more than scratch the surface of the current situation. Society along the border is deeply penetrated by bribery, and steeped in the volatile mixture of violence, murder, guns and drugs.

These measures stand no chance of being any more successful in the future than they have been in the past. There remains one clear alternative. If drugs were to be legalized, the money would evaporate, corruption would wither, and the cartels and their private armies would have to look elsewhere for a profitable purpose to which to put their talents. Nothing would be likely to pay as well as drug smuggling.

Cast your gaze back to 1933 and see what happened to the bootleggers and their henchmen. Legalization would transform life on the border with huge social gains, but it would take time. Government would have breathing space to tackle the seemingly insurmountable problems of gun control. Everyone would benefit. The price would be that any adult who wanted to could use drugs. This, though, would be no change, because that is the situation now. There would be massive savings for the police, the customs service, the Drug Enforcement Agency and the criminal justice system.

There is a further example of the insidious power of money to corrupt, which has only recently come to light. The US has in place federal banking laws designed to prevent money laundering, notably of drug money. The Wachovia Bank, which is now owned by Wells Fargo, has admitted laundering at least $110 million of Mexican cartel money, and failed to monitor a further unbelievable $420 billion of transactions. Drug dealers were able to use Wachovia accounts to buy planes, at least four of which were seized by the authorities loaded with 20,000 kilos of cocaine.[89]

This is very unlikely to be the last of this kind of story. It would be nice to regard banks as above such practices, and one has to wonder if these oversights were ill-judged commercial decisions, or whether they were criminal acts for which money changed hands. Either way, it is alarming to find banks involved in questionable or criminal activities, and it will do no good for the already tarnished reputation of the banking industry.

There is now incontrovertible evidence that drug money is funding international terrorist organizations. The word narco-terrorism was first used in 1983 in relation to attacks on Peru's drug enforcement police. Since the events of 11 September 2001, in New York and elsewhere, the term has come to mean any activity by groups or individuals which raise money from, or in some other way support, drug trafficking, in an effort to further or fund terrorist activity.

Look at almost any trouble spot in the world, and there is evidence of it. Colombia, Peru, Bolivia, Venezuela, Central America, Mexico and the Mexican-US border, the Caribbean, Northern Ireland (until recently), Spain, Turkey, the Middle East, Yemen, Afghanistan, Pakistan and West Africa have all seen militant criminal organizations funded by drug money. Drug-financed outrages are a constant threat to European and North American cities, and it is only a matter of time before they strike again. Efforts to counter these groups have, in some cases, been quite successful, but they have taken a long time, and cost numerous lives and vast amounts of money. While all the strategies devised include attempts to cut off their lifeblood – money – none of them seem to have considered the most obvious way to do this. If the price of cocaine and heroin were to fall dramatically these groups would be left destitute and impotent. That could be done by making drugs legal, and hence mere commodities, like sugar or wheat, trading at prices determined by the market.

Our focus now moves from the international to the domestic arena. For many the most attractive case for the legalization of drugs relates to its likely effect on the level and extent of drug-related crime. The whole relationship between drugs and crime is discussed in some detail in Chapter 5. Meanwhile, it remains an important argument in favour of legalization.

We have seen that illegal markets are inherently expensive, and that legally available drugs would be cheaper. It might even be that certain drugs would continue to be free, as is now the case in treatment centres run by Britain's National Health Service. Cheap or free drugs would no longer impose the necessity to acquire money by nefarious means, or to convert stolen goods to cash at a huge discount. The present 'multiplier effect' of quick sales of stolen goods would go into reverse, and disproportionately reduce the amount of acquisitive crime. It is certainly not being suggested that all criminal behaviour would cease, but the level of acquisitive crime would be likely to fall, particularly in the longer term. Since criminals are involved at all stages in the supply of illegal drugs at present, they would have to find some other field in which to practise their talents.

Evidence following the decriminalization of drugs in Portugal suggests that, while opportunistic street crime initially increased, the more premeditated and serious forms of theft or fraud reduced substantially.[90] The retail price of drugs has fallen since the change in the law, and this is likely to reduce crime in the long term. Legalization of drugs, and the introduction of controlled and regulated markets for drugs – a step which has not been taken in Portugal because decriminalization does not make drugs legal – would certainly reduce prices further, and hence to reduce or eliminate acquisitive crime.

The last several years have seen increasing use of the criminal justice system to deal with lesser drug offences. While nobody would suggest that drug dealers or traffickers should avoid the prescribed legal penalties, minor offences, such as possession, are not appropriately dealt with by the law. The courts in Britain now have powers to refer addicts for treatment, but these people take precedence over those who have referred themselves. This is an important issue because the latter group, being self-selected, are much more likely to get and remain abstinent, whereas those sent by the courts for treatment almost never stay clean.[91]

Places on treatment courses are limited, and one patient told the author that (a particular drug treatment unit) 'is quite useless because you wait forever. People are getting arrested on purpose so they can jump the queue. I contacted them and they told me to do the same if I didn't mind my name in the paper – but I did mind so I am still waiting.'[92]

Obviously, those most likely to benefit should be drawn into treatment, not those who are not ready to become abstinent. Countless judges have pointed out that little worthwhile can be achieved during a short prison sentence. Prison achieves nothing positive for drug offenders: it acts as neither deterrent nor corrective. Shockingly, many prisoners actually acquire their drug habit in prison. The original justification for the involvement of the criminal justice system in drug policy was solely to deter the use of drugs. It does not do that, and therefore has no place. Furthermore, many argue that the state has no just reason for punishing drug use. The policy of legalization recognizes that addiction is primarily a public health concern. This is in the starkest contrast to the situation in America, where over half a million prisoners convicted of non-violent, and often minor, drug offences are incarcerated at huge financial and social cost.

It cannot be argued that the illegality imposed by prohibition stops people using drugs, because it is not true. Quite apart from the fact that drugs are universally available in spite of prohibition, there have been at least two recent surveys of public attitudes in Britain which demonstrate, beyond any doubt, that neither illegality, nor the classification of an illegal drug, nor even the possibility of arrest and the threat of legal penalties, have any influence on the choice of drug to be used, and certainly has no deterrent effect.[93]

What prohibition does do, though, is to make many decent and otherwise law-abiding citizens, who happen to like a little cannabis or an occasional ecstasy tablet, into criminals. Figures from the 2009/10 British Crime Survey show that over a third of 16-59-year olds, or nearly 12 million people, admitted to having taken an illegal drug at some time, which made them all into technical criminals.[94] And much worse, the few who get caught and cautioned or prosecuted, will thereby have a criminal record, making future employment very much more difficult.

There are significant numbers of young people who have a criminal record for minor drug offences. The great majority of them are normal people who happen to like to take recreational drugs occasionally, like hundreds of thousands of their contemporaries, but had the ill luck to get caught in the wrong place at the wrong time. They do not see themselves as criminals, but having a criminal record blights their future lives. Husak argues that the harm done by conferring a criminal record is, in the great majority of cases, greater than the harm resulting from taking drugs. Many senior police officers are very aware of this and consequently loath to take action. Furthermore, they regard the policing of prohibition as a time-taking burden that makes them less able to concentrate on more important work.

We must also examine the costs of maintaining a policy of prohibition, and to see what the probable effects of legalization would be on this expenditure. These costs are very high. They are aggregated from the proportion of total costs of the police and customs service, and the administration of justice, prison and community programmes, attributable to drug offences. The figure for 2004/5 was £2 billion, or nearly four times the amount spent on drug treatment.[95]

In Britain it is estimated that illegal drug taking requires a workforce of about 5,000 customs officers, and 18,000 police officers, who are consequently not available for other duties. To this must be added the enormous cost borne by private individuals, retail shops, the insurance industry and various pockets of the public purse, collectively known as the victim costs of drug-related crime. This amounts to £9.7 billion annually.[96] We currently spend large amounts in other countries trying to prevent drugs reaching our shores – perhaps £500 million every year. It would be absurd to suggest that these costs would disappear, but they would fall, and a 'legalization dividend' would more than finance a major expansion in treatment programmes, and a great and necessary rise in their quality. It would also make our society a safer and more pleasant place in which to live. The comparable figure in the United States is about $50 billion every year.

The drug policy charity Transform, a think-tank which campaigns for workable co-existence with drugs, has examined the likely savings of moving from prohibition to a regulated market. Because of the uncertainties which might follow such a move, they have, for illustrative purposes, examined four different scenarios – a 50 per cent fall in drug taking, no change in use, a 50 per cent rise in use and a 100 per cent rise in use. They conclude that the net savings to tax payers, victims of crime, communities, the criminal justice system and drug users would be in the range of £13.9 billion, £10.8 billion, £7.7 billion and £4.6 billion for the four scenarios respectively.[97] A number of potential benefits, such as the tax which could be raised, are not costed and included because the uncertainties are too great. Many of the assumptions on which this work is based will be questioned, but if the figures are taken as illustrative only, they do demonstrate how expensive it is to retain the discredited and ineffective prohibition policy.

One of the most objectionable aspects of prohibition is that it is applied unfairly and disproportionately to minorities. In England and Wales in 2003/4, 14 per cent of those arrested for drug offences were white, and 78 per cent were black. Census figures showed that white people represented 89 per cent of the population and black people only 2 per cent. Furthermore, blacks were less likely than whites to be cautioned, and more likely to be charged, sentenced and imprisoned. Members of the black population were 7 times more likely to be arrested, and 14 times more likely to be imprisoned than their white peers, in spite of roughly similar rates of drug use.[98/99] In the US the situation is much the same. Even though white drug users outnumber blacks by 5 to 1, 63 per cent of all drug offenders admitted to state prisons for drug offences are black, and only 37 per cent are white. This is a shocking state of affairs.

Truth, honest behaviour and civil liberties are all threatened by prohibition. We have read in Chapter 3 some of the ridiculous and dishonest statements and claims made about drugs and drug users by the fanatics of prohibition. There is some evidence to suggest that, on both sides of the Atlantic, there are politicians who do not subscribe to the policy of prohibition, yet are reluctant to say so on the record, lest their constituents should cease to support them. In Britain there have been two notable exceptions in Mo Mowlem and Bob Ainsworth, both of whom were formerly ministers responsible for drug policy, and their honesty and candour is to be welcomed.

In America, the security and anti-drug bureaucracy has become so vast, and has been given so much money and such wide powers, that it is difficult to keep it accountable. The Internet posts many stories of outrageous abuse of power and disregard for basic civil liberties by employees of these agencies. The enormous sums of money generated by the illicit drug trade make some degree of corruption of law-enforcement inevitable. Even foreign policy can become perverted to serve the short-term purposes of the 'War on Drugs'. The United States finds itself supporting corrupt regimes simply because they profess a willingness to join the fight against drugs.

The illegality of prohibition has two further practical effects: people tend not to answer surveys or to tell the truth about their drug taking; and it makes some hold back from going into treatment. It is important to know how many drug users there are, and what they take, if policy and services are to be effectively planned and delivered. Furthermore, uncertain or inaccurate figures allow interested groups to misrepresent their arguments. Delay in presenting for treatment can be damaging, and it affects particularly the most vulnerable. For example, women who are single mothers fear that contact with officialdom of any sort might result in social services removing their child into care.

Political correctness has had the sad and regrettable effect of making doctors too hesitant to use heroin on the relatively rare occasions on which it really is indicated. There is an undeniable reluctance to use it because there is a perception that 'big brother' is on the staff of every hospital, and prohibition is responsible for this. It is a wonderful drug for those in the greatest pain and distress, and we are still permitted to prescribe it in Britain for this purpose. If we do not do so it will be said that we do not need it. 'Brompton's Mixture' has been a victim of the same squeamishness. It contained heroin, cocaine, gin and honey, and it used to be given to those who were suffering intolerably both physically and mentally, and were close to death.

We have seen that prohibition encourages the more extreme, and therefore dangerous, forms of drug use. Contact with dealers is risky, and therefore needs to be as 'effective' as possible in terms of buying the biggest buzz in the shortest time. The controlled and regulated markets envisaged under legalization would make available a wider range of less potent drugs which would suit the needs of many users in a freer and more relaxed environment. Exactly the same thing happened after the end of alcohol prohibition in America.

A regulated and legal market could impose a wide variety of controls on drug sales and usage. Everyone agrees that there should be age-limits for the purchase of drugs, which could be different according to the substance. There could be penalties for selling to those who were intoxicated. Sales could be dependent upon proof of identity, age or location of residence. It would be possible to keep a running total of drugs sold to an individual online, in order to identify those who might need treatment because they were using too much, or might be selling drugs to others.

If diversion were suspected, it would be possible to micro-tag drugs. These are microscopic tracers, which act like a barcode, and hence could identify the person to whom the drug was originally sold. Licensed outlets could be subject to sensible requirements, which, if infringed, would result in appropriate sanctions being applied. A system of licensing users could be introduced which was contingent upon certain levels of knowledge appropriate to the drugs to which the license gave access. And lastly, there could be controls on the location where drugs could be consumed, as there are today with smoking tobacco. These might differ according to the route by which drugs were used – whether they were taken by mouth, smoked or injected. There could be an almost infinitely flexible system of controlled access to drugs – a very far cry from the present situation under prohibition. Transform has considered these possibilities very carefully, and made very practical and workable suggestions, as we shall shortly see.

The legalization of all currently illegal drugs is a far-reaching and radical proposal that has many opponents. It is right that we should address their concerns. There is an obvious possibility that legalization might lead to an increase, even a considerable increase, in the number of drug users. Whether it would or would not is unknowable until it is tried, but there are pointers that permit us to make an educated guess.

Recent experience in Portugal since decriminalization of all drugs gives us the best clues available so far.[100] The consensus of opinion is that there has been a slight to moderate increase in overall reported drug use among young adults. However, it may not be quite as simple as that. The critics of decriminalization argue that it has resulted in a perception that illicit drug use is acceptable, which has caused an increase in use, particularly of cannabis.

Supporters argue that apparent increases may be spurious, and that they reflect increased and more truthful reporting because of the reduction in the stigma of drug use. The jury is still out on this important point. What does seem much clearer is that there has been a significant reduction in the number of problematic and injecting drug users, having very important health advantages, in that there has been a reduction in opiate-related deaths and in infectious diseases like Hepatitis C and HIV/AIDS. This important finding should reassure those who predict that legalization will lead to an increase in the more extreme forms of drug use.

A further objection to legalization is that domestic drug legislation throughout the world is an obligation placed upon all those governments that were signatories of the 1961 United Nations Single Convention, the 1971 Convention on Psychotropic Substances and the 1988 Convention against the illicit Traffic in

Narcotic Drugs. It is held that significant change in domestic drug law is impossible because it is constrained by these agreements. This is simply not true. Any country is free to repudiate such an agreement if it really becomes necessary, but there is in any case considerable room or manoeuvre within the existing framework. As we know, Portugal has decriminalized all drugs, and many other nations, including many states in America, have effectively decriminalized cannabis. It would be possible to revisit the wording of these conventions if enough countries wished to do so.

The most important consequence of legalization of drugs would be the nature of the market. There would no longer be a black market in drugs because they could be bought legally from those chemists, or other licensed outlets, which choose to sell them. And here lies the importance of legalizing all drugs because there will always be a criminal market in any illegal commodity. There could be a totally free market in which anyone could buy whatever they wanted without any constraint, but that is a theoretical notion which would gain little or no practical support, other than from a few academic philosophers or economists. It would probably lead to over-use and major hazards to health, and it would offer no protection to potential under-age users. It would also open the way for multinational pharmaceutical companies to advertise and promote recreational drugs, something that would be rigorously forbidden in a regulated market.

There are, in theory, a number of ways in which a regulated market could be organized. Transform has made a careful study of the options, published in a book entitled 'Blueprint for Regulation'.[101] This envisages five graduated mechanisms by which the supply of drugs could be regulated. The most restrictive is prescription by a doctor of a specified amount, which will have binding instructions about the dates on which the drugs are to be dispensed. There may also be other conditions attached, such as consumption in the pharmacy. This would be appropriate for drugs with the greatest potential for harm, such as heroin, other opiates, and crack cocaine, most especially if they are to be injected. It might also be that, subject to analysis of the results of pilot studies of drug consumption rooms, such prescriptions could only be dispensed in such a facility, and its use supervised to ensure safety.

Less harmful drugs could be on sale without a prescription from licensed pharmacies, in which perhaps there was a specially trained pharmacist. This would be appropriate for drugs like powdered cocaine, ecstasy and amphetamines sold to a named individual. Less restrictive still would be licensed sales, much in the same way as tobacco and alcohol are sold now. Next, there could be some drugs made available from licensed premises, for which a useful model is the coffee shops selling cannabis in Holland. This would include many pubs, subject to the acceptance by the landlord of the conditions of their license to sell drugs. And lastly the substances considered to pose little or no risk, like coffee and some painkillers, could be sold over the counter and freely available. However, such products would have to be of guaranteed quality, and appropriately labelled, where the vendor should be sufficiently knowledgeable to give advice when necessary. These are the views of one interested body, which has clearly thought about the problems very hard. Nevertheless, there will be other ideas, but Transform has put in place a framework with which others might work.

There are also flaws. For example, it is relatively simple to convert powdered cocaine into crack cocaine, and some users will certainly do this. But most will not because casual users of cocaine powder usually have no taste for crack. Furthermore, if it is made too arduous to obtain cocaine powder it will encourage an illicit market.

Another major concern is whether or not criminal markets in drugs would continue to exist. If the licensed price is inflated, they could. After all, cigarettes and alcohol in Britain can be bought at cheaper prices than apply in shops, from people who purchase goods in less heavily taxed countries, and import them illegally. But that opportunity is unlikely to be available to those who wish to sell drugs, or if it were then they would be dealing in cheap imported drugs of unknown strength and purity, and would be committing a crime by not paying the tax levied, and sooner or later arrested. There might possibly persist a small black market in which drugs were sold at prices higher than the legal market, to supply a few people who wanted to remain anonymous, or did not wish to accept whatever stigma might be attached to buying in licensed outlets.

The price of drugs is a very important issue. We know that illegal markets are expensive because they must take account of the inherent risks of violence and imprisonment. Drugs prepared or manufactured professionally would be cheaper, but it is a certainty, and appropriate, that the government will wish to tax legally sold drugs. The price set, therefore, must be well judged. It should be high enough to discourage profligate use, and low enough to ensure that undercutting by illegal suppliers would not be worthwhile. Nevertheless there are many factors that influence the price that users will pay for drugs, but price is very easy to adjust in the light of experience.

An argument used against legalization is that if drugs were made legal and the policy was found to be undesirable or worse, it would be impossible to retreat to the *status quo ante*. It is not impossible to reverse public policy. There is a recent and relevant precedent. In 1975, the Supreme Court of the State of Alaska ruled that any citizen should be permitted to possess up to a quarter of a pound of cannabis in his or her own home. Alaskans voted to re-criminalize cannabis possession in 1991, but in 2004 the Supreme Court reaffirmed its 1975 decision. In 2006, the Alaskan House approved a bill to criminalize cannabis once again, but the State was sued by the American Civil Liberties Union for an unconstitutional invasion of privacy. The new law was struck down, and it is now legal to possess up to one ounce of cannabis in your home. This vacillation is undesirable, but it has not made Alaska ungovernable, nor has it had any impact on the lives of the vast majority of Alaskans.

There is, though, no reason why there would be any need to reverse policy in such a dramatic way since there would have to be initial legislation to remove the legal punishments for possession which now apply. But that, in itself, would make little practical difference.

Those who continue to advocate prohibition have fears that there will be a sudden flood of drugs resulting in many more users, and much more chaotic and damaging forms of use. In reality, the availability of drugs will be controlled from the start by the kind of mechanisms referred to above. Furthermore, initially these will be very cautiously operated, and err on the side of over-regulation. There will be a great need to demonstrate to sceptics that their worst fears are unfounded. It would also be likely that legalization would be rolled out slowly, perhaps starting with cannabis.

There is already a lot of support for liberalizing access to this drug, which has been used by over 11 million Britons at some time. It might then be possible to introduce weaker and less harmful versions of other drugs, such as magic mushrooms rather than LSD, or poppy straw tea, which the current criminal market does not make available, for reasons already alluded to. Experience would be gained over months or even several years, which could guide changes in the controls, be they to further restrict availability, or to liberalize it. More radical or controversial proposals could be tested by pilot studies, as is currently the case with heroin treatment in drug consumption rooms. This incremental and circumspect approach, based on experience, is likely to evolve into effective and workable regulation.

However attractive this principle of regulated and controlled markets may be in theory, it is going to be an uphill struggle to get the necessary support from politicians. That is not, however, a reason not to try to persuade doubters. Indeed, it should spur on renewed efforts, for there are a few cracks appearing in the edifice of prohibition. And it is likely that the principles of prohibition will be challenged under Human Rights legislation at some point in the future. It might be that the likely effects of legalization on terrorism and international criminality prove to be a more attractive and acceptable justification for such a major change in policy. Whatever the off-the-record views of politicians may be, they will see the espousal of legalization as a political liability, but perhaps the much bigger international possibilities might defuse the domestic political unattractiveness. This possibility represents one of the most important choices ever offered to the leaders of our world, which could bring undreamed of benefits to hundreds, if not thousands, of millions of people right across the globe.

8 Making it Happen

It would be a major mistake to believe that far-reaching change in the way that society thinks about and treats illegal drugs will be easily achieved. However good may be the intellectual arguments in favour of legalization, we must acknowledge that as of now they appeal only to a minority of citizens. Furthermore, winning or losing a rational argument is not, at any rate initially, the issue. Years of unthinking prejudice and fear is a much tougher nut to crack.

Such attitudes have provided loyal support for the only policy which seemed possible and likely to work. But now society faces a different set of challenges because prohibition has failed utterly. It is a policy which has been tested to destruction, particularly in the United States, and there is no chance that it can be 'born again' with any prospect of success. The unthinking, and occasionally far-from-silent majority, must still be seen as a major obstacle to progress. They cannot be ignored until there is a major shift in sentiment, yet sentiment is on the move.

In an earlier chapter we identified how drugs had been consciously and systematically demonized. It was an effective strategy for the prohibitionists. Its effect was to 'set aside' the problem of illegal drugs from any of the other policy discussions of current interest to society. Any arguments which might be advanced in favour of anything other than prohibition were denied legitimacy because the subject was, it was alleged, touched by dark and dangerous forces, if not by the devil himself.

Prejudice on the subject of drugs exists in all sections of society. If you engage someone in conversation in any of the thousands of pubs serving the urban areas of our cities, forthright views are likely to be expressed. But they often see no connection between drugs and the fact that they themselves may smoke twenty or more cigarettes a day, and drink two or three pints of beer of an evening. You will find it in the coffee shops and hairdressers of middle class towns, where it is assumed that anyone who takes heroin is a write-off, and will never again become a responsible member of society. There are numerous readers of the *Daily Mail* and the *Daily Telegraph*, who are treated to a drip-feed of rabid propaganda by probably well-meaning but deeply ignorant and usually right-wing journalists. Yet the smokers and drinkers in our pubs are today offered other delights, including in many, powdered cocaine and cannabis. These drugs do a brisk trade, particularly at the weekends in the under forty-five age group.

Mrs Tunbridge Wells and her friends are having to face the completely shattering discovery that their beloved child has a heroin habit. This can turn a parent's world upside down, usually because they are so unprepared. But, had they been in touch with the social world of the under thirty-fives, they would have discovered that it is normal to use recreational drugs at the weekends, and very often to drink less alcohol than their parents. Cannabis, ecstasy, Valium and perhaps a little LSD are the staples. Such behaviour is unremarkable and largely harmless. But there are risks. These are known by those who take these drugs, for they are usually very knowledgeable, and certainly know a lot more about drugs than their parents, or even than their doctors, whose ignorance and hostility towards drug users is often shocking.

Age is an important issue. Many parents of children now in or approaching their late thirties or forties will not, themselves, have lived in a society in which drugs were commonplace. There either were no drugs when they were young, or they smoked a little herbal cannabis or 'pot'. It was weak stuff, and it caused a good deal of giggling and very little harm. It was an adventure – even a rite of passage – among the more adventurous. But they will have no familiarity with serious addiction, and consequently no knowledge of the signs in one of their children that all may not be well. When and if they have to face this reality their life will never be the same again.

Understandably the disastrous effects that heroin can have on the lives of its users, and the premature deaths which it sometimes causes, loom large in the common perceptions which the uninitiated have about drugs. In truth, most who fall under the spell of heroin give it up. A few die young from overdoses, almost always because they inject it intravenously. But the common notion that heroin addiction leads inexorably to social ostracism and dereliction is simply wrong. There are thousands of young people to bear witness to this.

Another common belief is that drugs ruin health. Even heroin is remarkably innocuous physically, though it has catastrophic consequences for the lives of users. Illegal drugs are no different from prescribed drugs in that they both can have undesirable side-effects.

There is a common supposition that addicts have an addictive personality, and that this may have some genetic basis. There is very little to support this theory. The current view is that addiction is the result of a complex interaction of social, psychological, biological and environmental influences. It may well be that addicts are more inclined to be risk-takers than others. Drug taking is certainly a profoundly self-indulgent behaviour in which instant gratification is the objective. It is also an immature behaviour, and giving up drugs frequently coincides with the process of growing up.

One last misconception must be laid to rest. It is quite impossible to make someone give up drugs against their will – unless they are incarcerated in a drug-free environment. Addicts will become abstinent when *they* decide that they have had enough of drugs and the druggy world. It will be *their* decision, although, of course, they may be influenced by many things in reaching this decision.

Drug taking and addiction are best freed from taboo status. Many of the thousands of families whose lives have been touched by the problem are loath to talk about it. Exposing the issues will start to change attitudes. A generation ago, the subject of cancer was only mentioned in hushed tones. Talking about it openly and in a matter-of-fact way has changed everybody's perception of this widespread disease. People now know much more and hear about successful treatment, whereas before they had heard only of the failures. Knowledge and accurate information freely discussed defeat fear, ignorance and prejudice.

If you 'Google' *heroin* you have instant access to about 43,100,100 citations. *Drug addiction* produces about 52,100,000 references, and *heroin addiction* about 2,810,000 (accessed 7 September 2011). There is a vast amount of information out there, much of it indigestible and often unintelligible. Some is from genuinely public interest organizations, often sponsored by government, such as the 'ask FRANK' site, which will also put you in touch with telephone help-lines and an opportunity to speak to a well-informed and sympathetic voice. Much information is provided by somewhat more alternative interests, sponsored by bodies selling advice or some other service, such as detoxification. Some have other agendas which are not immediately apparent. For example, Narconon, a charitable organization providing drug treatment services, is affiliated to the Church of Scientology. Most of the books about addiction and drug taking fall into one of two groups: those aimed at professionals in the field, or personal accounts of drug taking experiences.

It is common for a parent to turn to a general practitioner for help. This can be really helpful, and the opportunity to voice fears and anger can be invaluable. Unfortunately, there are many GPs who will not offer much, if any, assistance, and some who are so antagonistic to the world of drugs that they will not even discuss the subject. I was told by a patient who had graduated from street heroin to methadone, and then to a small and diminishing dose of codeine, that his GP had said to him 'the sooner you lot take an overdose and kill yourselves, the better'.

I argue that legalization of all illegal drugs is a necessary step to the creation of a regulated and controlled market, run and taxed by government authority. Only in this way will illegal and uncontrolled markets run by criminals be made to wither and die. While this would be major step in the right direction, most emphatically do not suggest that it would solve the problem of drug abuse. The best we can hope for is to ameliorate some of its worst aspects. We may be able to whittle away at its more pernicious characteristics. We can abandon the search for the magic bullet – there never will be one. Let us concentrate all our efforts on those aspects of the total problem we judge to be the most important. In this light should the plea for legalization be seen.

Many will regard legalization as being a very dangerous step, even catastrophic. But in reality, it is a first step towards addressing one of the most worrying aspects of society's interaction with these substances. If and when we have controlled access to drugs from a legal, logical and regulated market, we can move on to the next step; to search for more effective ways of persuading young people to be cautious about experimenting with drugs (if they could get hold of any). Drugs will have lost their allure, being no more forbidden than, say, alcohol.

It is possible to bring people of opposing views together for useful discourse. A recent publication by Demos and the UK Drug Policy Commission on the subject of controlling legal highs has shown how fruitful this approach can be.[102]

Here lies the value of parents of addicts, who have read up as much as they can, and learned from their experiences both with their child and with those who are treating them, to talk freely and authoritatively whenever the opportunity arises. So also can ex-addicts make a contribution, if they have the courage to do so. It surely will lead to heated debate, but facts and experience are powerfully persuasive. Public opinion on legalization is on the move, and in one direction – in support of it: something of a groundswell in perception. Observers of the drug scene cannot fail to notice that there are now more column inches and airtime than ever before devoted to consideration of the issue. The tone has changed too. Championed by a few journalists, like Simon Jenkins and Mary Ann Sieghart, for some years there has been relentless argument for a new and more rational approach, including a radical change in the way in which the law treats drugs possession. We read very recently that a number of public-spirited celebrities have petitioned the Prime Minister to decriminalize possession.[103] Such actions are welcome, and will motivate others. Decriminalization may be a step in the right direction, but my argument is that only legalization of all drugs would reap the real benefits consequent upon having a regulated and controlled market.

The Liberal Democrats, partners in government, will have debated the motion to legalize at their Party conference in September 2011. There is reason to believe that Downing Street would like to see some progress made with these difficult issues: a committee, or even a Royal Commission, to look into the workings of the 1971 Misuse of Drugs Act, and to make recommendations, would be a most progressive move for the government to take. This is unlikely to happen without support both in Parliament and the country for radical change. Without such backing, a government would be wary of this controversial debate. The assumption persists that prohibitionists are in a substantial majority. Polls are indicating that change is afoot. It is important to know what level of support a move to legalization would enjoy, both among the general public, and among members of Parliament, so that, when the time comes, the ground is well prepared, and the chances of enacting radical change are maximized.

Bob Ainsworth, a former minister with responsibility for drug policy, has publicly declared that prohibition is a failure and not the right way 'to go'. So too did the late Mo Mowlem, when she had similar responsibilities. There are other members of Parliament who will admit in private that they have grave doubts about the direction of drug policy. Very few, however, will make such statements on the record. They fear alienating their voters, de-selection and hostile media comment. It is now imperative to get the closet legalizers out into the open. The brooding sense of moral panic about illegal drugs must also be shown up for what it is.

Both inside Parliament and outside, opportunities are growing for fact finding and debate. An All-Party Parliamentary Group on Drug Policy Reform, chaired by Baroness Meacher, a now convinced and effective advocate of radical reform, is attracting impressive membership. A British Medicinal Cannabis Register aims to shed real light on the legitimacy of cannabis for medicinal purposes: an important subject that requires serious and rigorous study. Derived from cannabis, Sativex, a licensed drug, has beneficial effects on the muscle spasms of multiple sclerosis. This subject has not been well-served by the ultra-relaxed situation in many states in America, where some doctors will issue the necessary certificate of 'medical need', for a fee. This is in stark contrast to the rigidly prohibitionist policies of the recent past. One can't help but feel that the US government is moving slowly away from the excesses of the 'War on Drugs'. Legalization must be introduced by multi-lateral agreement, simultaneously, and in such a global manoeuvre the participation of the US is central.

Stirrings on the international front are at last perceptible. The recently formed Global Commission on Drug Policy has issued a report to the UN expressing concern about the corruption and violence which illegality confers and calling for new thinking.[104] Although signed by an impressive list of international luminaries, including Kofi Annan, Paul Volker, and the former presidents of several South American countries, by itself it will hardly provoke international action. Nevertheless, steady pressure from experienced and respected political figures will help to keep the subject high on the political agenda. These reports do provide responsible journalists with copy. It is encouraging that recent press comment is mostly trying to push Cameron and Obama into more effective and radical action.

Conversely, several press articles, while accepting that prohibition has been a total failure, advocate caution on the grounds of the dangers of those drugs deemed fit for decriminalization. One such was a personal and impassioned plea by Patrick Cockburn,[105] that the risks of smoking cannabis were being ignored. His son, a cannabis smoker, had become schizophrenic. He quotes evidence which few would dispute, but some would say that he had the balance wrong. For example, he did not mention that there is now a genetic test to determine if an individual will be susceptible to psychotic illness from the regular use of cannabis. Evidence has been considered by the Advisory Council on the Misuse of Drugs and come to different conclusions about the risk level.[106]

Seventy-nine years ago, John D Rockefeller Junior, an impassioned advocate of temperance, who had spent great sums of his own money lobbying for the prohibition of alcohol, wrote a letter to the *New York Times*. In it he admitted the error of his investment. He had not changed his views on the evils of alcohol. But he insisted that it was essential to lift prohibition, 'to restore public respect for the law.' '[When] the Eighteenth Amendment was passed', he went on, 'I earnestly hoped – with a host of advocates of temperance – that it would be generally supported by public opinion' and that abstinence from alcohol would eventually take hold. 'That this has not been the result but rather that drinking generally has increased, that the speakeasy has replaced the saloon, not only for unit but probably two-fold if not three-fold; that a vast army of lawbreakers has been recruited and financed on a colossal scale; that many of our best citizens, piqued at what they regarded as an infringement of their private rights, have openly and unabashed(ly) disregarded the Eighteenth Amendment; that as an inevitable result respect for all law has greatly lessened; that crime has increased to an unprecedented degree – I have slowly reluctantly come to believe.'

He commented that any 'benefits' from the Eighteenth Amendment were 'more than outweighed by the evils that had developed and flourished since its adoption, evils which, unless promptly checked' were 'likely to lead to conditions unspeakably worse than those which prevailed before.'[107]

This voice, speaking to us from three generations ago, is eerily relevant today. Rockefeller's moral authority was such that his letter eventually led to the repeal of prohibition. We need men and women like him today on both sides of the Atlantic. Maybe they are beginning to raise their voices. Let us hope that the right people are listening.

SUGGESTED FURTHER READING

General interest

The Pursuit of Oblivion. (2001). Richard Davenport-Jones. London: Weidenfeld and Nicholson.

Opium and the People. (1999). Virginia Berridge. London: Free Association Books.

In the Arms of Morpheus. (2001). Barbara Hodgson. Buffalo: Firefly Books.

Opium and the Romantic Imagination. (1968). Althea Hayter. London: Faber and Faber.

High Society: Mind Altering Drugs in History and Culture. (2010). Mike Jay. London: Thames and Hudson.

Amexica: War Along the Borderline (2010). Ed Vulliamy. London: The Bodley Head.

Black Vinyl, White Powder. (2001). Simon Napier-Bell. London: Ebury Press.

Waiting for the Man. (2003). Harry Shapiro. London: Helter Skelter Publishing.

The Shaman. (1995). Piers Vitebsky. London: Duncan Baird Publishing.

Foreign Mud. (1946). Maurice Collins. New York: New Directions Books.

Books by users

Confessions of an English Opium Eater. (1821). Thomas De Quincey. Oxford: Oxford World Classics.

Junky (2008). William S Burroughs. London: Penguin Modern Classics.

How to Stop Time: Heroin from A to Z. (1999). Ann Marlow. London: Virago Press.

The Heroin Users. (1987). Tam Stuart. London: Harper Collins.

Books about drugs

Heroin Century. (2002). Tom Carnwath and Ian Smith. London: Routledge.

A Brief History of Cocaine. (1997). Steven Karch. Bocca Raton: CRC Press.

The Science of Marijuana. (2008). Leslie Iversen. Oxford: OUP.

Speed, Ecstasy, Ritalin: the Science of Amphetamines. (2006). Leslie Iversen. Oxford: OUP

Shroom: a cultural history of the Magic Mushroom. (2006). Andy Letcher. London: Faber and Faber.

Storming Heaven. (1987). Jay Stevens. New York: Grove Press.

The politics of drugs

Heroin addiction Care and Control: The British System 1916 to 1984. (2002). H B Spear, edited by Joy Mott. London: DrugScope.

Drug War Heresies. (2001). Robert MacCoun and Peter Reuter. Cambridge: CUP.

The Politics of Heroin: CIA Complicity in the Global Drug Trade. (2003). Alfred W McCoy. Chicago: Lawrence Hill Books.

Shooting up: Counterinsurgency and the War on Drugs. (2010). Vanda Felbab-Brown. Washington: Brookings Institution Press.

The Politics of Cocaine. (2010). William Marcy. Chicago: Lawrence Hill Books.

The Globalisation of Addiction. (2008). Bruce K Alexander. Oxford: OUP.

The Legalization of Drugs: For and Against. (2005). Douglas Husak and Peter Marnette. Cambridge: CUP.

After the War on Drugs: Blueprint for Regulation. (2009). Bristol: Transform Drug Policy Foundation.

REFERENCES

1   Rudgley, R., *The Alchemy of Culture: Intoxicants in Society*, London: British Museum Press, 1993, p. 25.

2   United Nations Office on Drugs and Crime, (UNODC), *World Drug Report 2010*, Vienna: United Nations Publication, 2010, p. 15.

3   Berridge, V., *Opium and the People*, London: Free Association Books, 1999, Ch. 4.

4   Ibid, p. 97.

5   Nutt, D. et al., *Development of a rational scale to assess the harm of drugs of potential misuse*, Lancet, no. 369, 24 March, 2007.

6   Stewart, T., *The Heroin Users*, London: Pandora, 1996, p. 22.

7   Ibid, p. 36.

8   Marlowe, A., *How to Stop Time: Heroin from A to Z*, London: Virago Press, 1996.

9   Everitt, B., *Addiction*, Cambridge Alumni Magazine, No. 52, p. 2, Cambridge: University Development Office, 2007.

10 Hay, G., Gannon, M., MacDougall, J., Millar, T., Eastwood, C., and McKeganey N., "Local and national estimates of the prevalence of opiate use and/or crack cocaine use, 2004/5" In: Singleton N, Murray R and Tinsley C (eds.) *Measuring different aspects of problem drug use: methodological developments*, Home Office Online Report 16/06. London: Home Office, 2007.

11 'Drug Misuse Declared: Findings from the 2009-10 British Crime Survey.' (2010). Statistical Bulletin 13/10. London: Home Office. p. 6.

12 Orr, J and Goswami, N. (2005). *The Daily Telegraph*. 5 November.

13 Chittenden, M. (2000). 'UK: Cocaine found inside the Houses of Parliament'. *The Sunday Times*. 5 November.

14 'Cocaine traces in EU Parliament'. (2005). BBC News 24. 15 July. http://news.bbc.co.uk/l/hi/world/Europe/4685693.stm

15 *The Times*. October 11, 2006.

16 WHO/UNICRI Cocaine Project. (1995). Geneva. Leaked, and published on the internet 2009.

17 Report of the Departmental Committee on Morphine and Heroin Addiction (The Rolleston Committee). (1926). London: HMSO.

18 Report of the Interdepartmental Committee (The first Brain Committee). (1961). Ministry of Health and Department for Health in Scotland. London: HMSO.

19 'Drug Addiction: the second report of the Interdepartmental Committee (The second Brain Committee).' (1965). Ministry of Health and Department for Health in Scotland. London: HMSO

20 Hospital Memorandum – HM (67) 16. (1967). Ministry of Health.

London: HMSO.

21 Spear HB. (2002). 'Heroin addiction care and control: the British system.' Ed. Mott, J. London: DrugScope.

22 Report by the Advisory Committee in Drug Dependence (The Wooton Report). (1968). London: Home Office.

23 Spear HB. (2002). 'Heroin addiction care and control: the British system.' Editor – Mott J. London: DrugScope.

24 'Tackling Drug Misuse: a summary of the government's strategy.' (1985, 1986, 1988). London: Home Office.

25 'Treatment and Rehabilitation.' (1982). Advisory Council on the Misuse of Drugs. London: HMSO.

26 Dalrymple T. (2007). 'Junk Medicine: Doctors, Lies and the Addiction Bureaucracy.' Petersfield: Harriman House.

27 Report of the Medical Working Group on Drug Dependence. (1984). 'Guidelines of good clinical practice in the treatment of drug misuse.' London: HMSO.

28 Drug Misuse and Dependency Working Party. (1991). 'Drug Misuse and Dependency – Guidelines on Clinical Management.'

29 'Drug Misuse and Dependence – Guidelines on Clinical Management.' (1999). Department of Health, The Scottish Office, Department of Health Welsh Office, Department of Health and social Services, Northern Ireland. London: HMSO.

30 'Drug Misuse and Dependence: UK Guidelines on Clinical Management.' (2007). London: Department of Health (England), the Scottish Government, Welsh Assembly government and Northern Ireland Executive.

31 'AIDS and drug misuse, Parts 1 and 2.' (1988, 1989). Advisory Council on the Misuse of Drugs. Department of Health. London: HMSO.

32 Task Force of Review Services for Drug Misusers: Report of an Independent Review of Drug Treatment services in England. (1996). London: Department of Health.

33 'Tackling Drugs Together: a Strategy for England 1995-1998.' (1995). HM Government. London: HMSO.

34 "Tackling Drugs to build a better Britain: the government's ten year strategy for tackling drug misuse." (1998). HM Government. London: HMSO.

35 'Drugs: Protecting Families and Communities. The 2008 Drug Strategy.' (2008). HM Government. London: HMSO.

36 'Cannabis: Classification and Public Health' (2007). Advisory Council on the Misuse of Drugs. London: Home Office.

37 Godfrey C, Stewart D and Glossop M. (2004). 'Economic analysis of costs and consequences of the treatment of drug misuse: 2-year outcome data from the National Treatment Outcome Research Study (NTORS).' Addiction. 99. 697-707

38 Rydell, C. and Everingham, S. (1994). 'Controlling cocaine: supply vs

demand programmes.' www.rand.org/pubs/monograph_reports/MR331/index2.html

39   *The Week.* (2003). 1 March.

40   'Blueprint Drugs Education: The response of pupils and parents to the programme.' Executive Summary. (2009). London: Home Office.

41   Mo, B.P. and Way, E.L. (1966). 'Assessment of inhalation as a mode of administration of heroin by addicts.' *Journal of Pharmacology and Therapeutics.* 154. 142-151.

42   Walker, S. (2011). 'Krokodil: the drug that eats Junkies'. *The Independent.* 22 June.

43   'Prescribe more free heroin: Birt's secret advice to ministers.' (2006). February 9. *The Guardian.*

44   Matrix Knowledge Group. (2007). 'The illicit drug trade in the United Kingdom.' London: Home Office Online Report 20/07, p. 18.

45   Advisory Council on the Misuse of Drugs. (2002). 'The classification of Cannabis under the Misuse of Drugs Act 1971.' London: Home Office.

46   Advisory Council on the Misuse of Drugs. (2005). 'Further consideration of cannabis under the Misuse of Drugs Act 1971.' London: Home Office.

47   Royal Society of Arts Commission on Illegal Drugs, Communities and Public Policy. (2006).
      YouGov Survey Results. www.rsadrugscommission.org

48   'Tackling Drugs to build a better Britain: the government's ten year strategy for tackling drug misuse.' (1998). HM Government. London: HMSO.

49   Stevens, A., 'Britain's drug policy will not improve until we are bold enough to experiment'. *The Observer,* 5 Sept 2010. www.guardian.co.uk/world/2010/sep/05/portugal-uk-drugs-decriminalisation

50   Degenhart, L., and 21 others. (2008). 'Towards a Global View of Alcohol, Tobacco, Cannabis, and Cocaine use: findings from the WHO World Mental Health Surveys.' PLOS Medicine, Volume 5, Number 7, e141. Doi:10.1371/journal.pmed.0050141

51   Matrix Knowledge Group. (2007). 'The illicit drug trade in the United Kingdom.' Home Office Online Report 20/07, p. 22.

52   Hickman, M., Higgins, V., Hope, V., Bellis, M., Tilling, K., Walker. A. and Henry, J. (2004). 'Injecting drug use in Brighton, Liverpool and London: best estimates of prevalence and coverage of public health indicators.' Journal of Epidemiology and Community Health. 58, pp. 766-771.

53   'Drug Misuse Declared: Findings from the 2009-10 British Crime Survey.' (2010). Statistical Bulletin 13/10. London: Home Office, p. 20.

54   Hay, G., Gannon, M., MacDougal, J., Millar, T., Eastwood, C. and McKegany, N. (2007). 'National and regional estimates of the prevalence of opiate use and/or crack cocaine use: a summary of key findings.' Home Office Online Report 21/07. London: Home Office.

55   'Drug Misuse Declared: Findings from the 2009-10 British Crime Survey.' (2010). Statistical Bulletin 13/10. London: Home Office, p.11.

56   ibid

57   Advisory Council on the Misuse of Drugs. (2010). 'Report on the consideration of cathinones.' London: Home Office.

58   'Drug Misuse Declared: Findings from the 2010-11 British Crime Survey.' (2011). Statistical Bulletin 12/11. London: Home Office.

59   UNODC. World Drug Report 2010. Vienna: United Nations Office of Drugs and Crime.

60   Ibid. p. 12.

61   Ibid. p. 20.

62   Ibid. p. 162.

63   Ibid. p. 16.

64   Ibid. p. 18.

65   Prime Minister's Strategy Unit Drugs Report: 'Phase one – Understanding the issues' (2003), p. 73.

66   UNODC. World Drug Report 2010. Vienna: United Nations Office of Drugs and Crime, p. 21.

67   Ibid. p. 20.

68   Ibid. p. 67.

69   Hales, G. et al, (2006). 'Gun crime: the market in and use of illegal firearms.' Home Office Research Study, 298.

70   Birdwell, J., Chapman, J. and Singleton, N. (2011). 'Taking Drugs seriously: a Demos and UK Drug Policy Commission report on legal highs' London: Demos.

71   Hough, M. and Mayhew, P. (1985). 'Taking account of Crime: key findings from the 1984 British Crime Survey.' Home Office Research Study. Londin: Home Office.

72   Coid, J. and Carvell, A. (2000). 'The impact of methadone treatment on drug misuse and crime' Research Findings No 12. London: Home Office.

73   'Understanding drugs, alcohol and crime.' Bennett T and Holloway K. (2005). Oxford: OUP.

74   Parker, H., Bakx, K. and Newcombe, R., (1988). 'Living with Heroin' Milton Keynes: Open University Press.

75   Hales, G. et al. (2006). 'Gun crime: the market in and use of illegal firearms.' Home Office Research Study, 298.

76   Glossop, M., Marsden, J., Stewart, D., and Rolfe, A., (2000). 'Reductions in acquisitive crime and drug use after treatment of addiction problems: one-year follow-up outcomes' Drug and Alcohol Dependence. 58, pp. 197-204.

77   Godfrey, C., Eaton, G., McDougal, C. and Culyer, A., (2002). 'The economic and social costs of Class A drug use in England and Wales, 2000' Home Office Research Study 249. London: Home Office.

78   Brand, S. and Price, R., (2000). 'The economic and social costs of crime' Home Office Research Study 217. London: Home Office.

79   Gordon, L., Tinsley, L., Godfrey, C. and Parrott, S., (2006). 'The economic and social costs of Class A drug use in England and Wales, 2003/4' In:

Singleton, N., Murray, R. and Tinsley, C. eds., 'Measuring different aspects of problem drug use: methodological developments." Home Office Online Report 16/06. London: Home Office.

80 Ramsey, M. ed., (2003). *'Prisoners' drug use and treatment: seven research studies'* Home Office Research Study 267. London: Home Office.

81 Hughes, C. E. and Stevens, A. (2010). *'What can we learn from the Portuguese decriminalisation of drugs?'* British Journal of Criminology. Doi:10.1093/bjc/azk 083

82 UNODC. *World Drug Report 2010.* Vienna: United Nations Office on Drugs and Crime, pp. 237-40.

83 UNODC. Annual Report 2008. Vienna: United Nations Office on Drugs and Crime.

84 Ibid., pp. 243-4.

85 Szasz, T., *'Our right to Drugs: the case for a free market'.* (1992). Syracuse University Press.

86 Husak, D. & De Marnoffe, P., *'Legalize This!'* (2002). London: Verso.

87 Bennett, W. J., Dilulio, J. J., and Walters, J. P., (1996). *'Body Count: Moral Poverty and how to win America's war against crime and Drugs'* New York: Simon and Schuster.

88 Vulliamy, E. (2010). *'AmexicaWar Along the Borderline'*, The Bodley Head, p. xx.

89 Ibid. p. 302.

90 Hughes, C. E. and Stevens, A., (2010). *'What can we learn from the Portuguese decriminalisation of drugs?'* British Journal of Criminology. Doi:10.1093/bjc/azk 083

91 Cuppleditch, L. and Evans, W., (2005). *'Re-offending of adults: results from the 2002 cohort'* Home Office Statistical Bulletin 25/05. London: Home Office.

92 Personal communication to the author.

93 *'Drugs – facing the fact.'* (2007). Report of the Royal Society of Arts Commission on Illegal drugs, Communities and Public Policy. London: Royal Society of Arts.

94 2009/10 British Crime Survey

95 Reuter, P. and Stevens, A., (2007). *'An analysis of UK Drug Policy'* London: UKDPC, p. 52.

96 Godfrey, C., Stewart, D. and Glossop, M., (2004). *'Economic analysis of costs and consequences of the treatment of drug misuse: 2-year outcome data from the National Treatment Outcome Research Study (NTORS)'* Addiction. 99, pp. 697-707

97 *'A Comparison of the Cost-effectiveness of the Prohibition and Regulation of Drugs'* Bristol: Transform Drug Policy Foundation.

98 Barclay, G., Munley, A. and Munton, T., (2005). *'Statistics on Race and the Criminal Justice System: an overview of the complete statistics 2003-4'* Criminal Justice Race Unit. London: Home Office.

99   Aust, R. and Smith, N., (2003). '*Ethnicity and drug use: Key findings from the 2001-02 British Crime Survey*'. Findings 209. London: Home Office.

100   Hughes, C. E. and Stevens, A., (2010). '*What can we learn from the Portuguese decriminalisation of drugs?*' British Journal of Criminology. Doi:10.1093/bjc/azk 083

101   '*After the War on Drugs: Blueprint for Regulation*' (2009). Bristol: Transform Drug Policy Foundation.

102   Birdwell, J., Chapman, J. and Singleton, N., (2011). '*Taking Drugs Seriously: a Demos and UK Drug Policy Commission Report on Legal Highs.*' London: Demos.

103   Shakespeare, S., 'A war on drugs is a battle we can never win.' (2011). *Evening Standard.* 3 June

104   Global Commission on Drug Policy (2011) www.globalcommissionondrugs.org/Commission

105   Cockburn, P., (2011). 'Cannabis can alter your mind. Just ask my son, Henry.' *The Independent on Sunday*, 5 June.

106   Advisory Council on the Misuse of Drugs. (2008). '*Cannabis: classification and Public Health*' London: Home Office.

107   Quoted in: O'Grady, M. A. (2011). 'More calls for a drug war cease-fire.' *The Wall Street Journal*, 6 June.